POKÉMON™

CLASSIC COLLECTOR'S HANDBOOK

I0963090

OFFICIAL GUIDE TO THE FIRST 151 POKÉMON

SCHOLASTIC INC.

Special thanks to Silje Watson

ISBN 978-1-338-15823-6

10 9 8 7   20 21

Designed by Kay Petronio

Printed in the U.S.A.   40

This edition first printing, January 2017

Contents

Welcome, Trainers!

Congratulations on your newest catch—the Pokémon Classic Collector's Handbook! This book has been updated and upgraded just for you.

YOUR MISSION: To collect and train as many Pokémon as you can. You'll start your journey by choosing one of three Pokémon . . .

Bulbasaur

Charmander

Squirtle

Once you have your first Pokémon, you can catch other Pokémon—and battle other Pokémon!

The key to success in raising, battling, and evolving your Pokémon is staying informed. Information about each Pokémon's type, species, height, and weight can make all the difference in Gym battles, in the wild, and anywhere else you might meet Pokémon. This book will also tell you how each Pokémon evolves and which moves it uses.

So get ready, Trainers: Soon you'll be ready to master almost any Pokémon challenge! To keep learning, just *turn the page . . .*

What Are Pokémon?

Pokémon are creatures that come in all shapes, sizes, and personalities. Some live in oceans; others in caves, old towers, rivers, or tall grass. Trainers can find, capture, train, trade, collect, and use Pokémon in battle against their rivals in the quest to become top Pokémon Trainers.

This book contains 151 known species of Pokémon. For most species, there are many individual Pokémon. Some are very common, like Pidgey and Rattata. You can find them almost anywhere. Others, like Articuno, are classified as Legendary Pokémon and are extremely rare.

Each individual Pokémon has its own personality. For example, there are a lot of Pikachu, but Ash has a very special one who travels with him on all his adventures.

A Trainer's goal is to catch and befriend Pokémon in the wild, and then train them to battle one another. Pokémon do not get seriously hurt in battle. If they are defeated, they faint, and then return to their Poké Balls to rest and be healed. A Trainer's job is to take good care of his or her Pokémon.

How to Use This Book

This book will provide the basic stats and facts you need to know to start your Pokémon journey. Here's what you'll discover about each Pokémon:

TYPE
Each Pokémon has a type, and some even have two! (Pokémon with two types are called dual-type Pokémon.) Every Pokémon type comes with advantages and disadvantages.

DESCRIPTION
Knowledge is power! Pokémon Trainers have to know their stuff. Find out everything you need to know about your Pokémon here.

HOW TO SAY IT
When it comes to Pokémon pronunciation, it's easy to get tongue-tied! There are many Pokémon with unusual names, so we'll help you sound them out. Soon you'll be saying Pokémon names so perfectly, you'll sound like a professor!

HEIGHT AND WEIGHT
How does each Pokémon measure up? Find out by checking its height and weight stats. And remember, good things come in all shapes and sizes. It's up to every Trainer to work with his or her Pokémon and play up its size.

POSSIBLE MOVES
Every Pokémon has its own unique combination of moves. Before you hit the battlefield, we'll tell you all about each Pokémon's awesome attacks. And don't forget, with a good Trainer, they can always learn more!

EVOLUTION
If your Pokémon has an evolved form or pre-evolved form, we'll show you its place in the chain and how it evolves.

TYPE: W

With its ae
Squirtle's
quickly. It

HOW TO SAY I
IMPERIAL HE
METRIC HEIG

POSSIBLE MO
Bubble, Bite
Skull Bash,

EVOLUTION

Squir

(20)

#007

Squirtle
TINY TURTLE POKÉMON

POKÉDEX
NUMBER

SPECIES

CATEGORY
All Pokémon belong to
a certain category.

...amic shape and grooved surface,
...elps it cut through the water very
...ffers protection in battle.

...IR-tul
...08"   IMPERIAL WEIGHT: 19.8 lbs.
...   METRIC WEIGHT: 9.0 kg

...ckle, Tail Whip, Water Gun, Withdraw,
...d Spin, Protect, Water Pulse, Aqua Tail,
...Defense, Rain Dance, Hydro Pump

...Wartortle › Blastoise

Curious
about what
Pokémon types
you'll spot on your
journey? Find out
more about types
on the next
page . . .

Guide to Pokémon Types

Type is the key to unlocking a Pokémon's power. A Pokémon's type can tell you a lot about it—from where to find it in the wild to the moves it'll be able to use on the battlefield. For example, Water-type Pokémon usually live in lakes, oceans, and rivers and use moves like Bubble and Hydro Pump.

A clever Trainer should always consider type when picking a Pokémon for a match, because type shows a Pokémon's strengths and weaknesses. For example, a Fire-type may melt an Ice-type, but against a Water-type, it might find it's the one in hot water. And while a Water-type usually has the upper hand in battle with a Fire-type, a Water-type move would act like a sprinkler on a Grass-type Pokémon. But when that same Grass-type is battling a Fire-type, it just might get scorched.

The Pokémon in this book have seventeen different types . . .

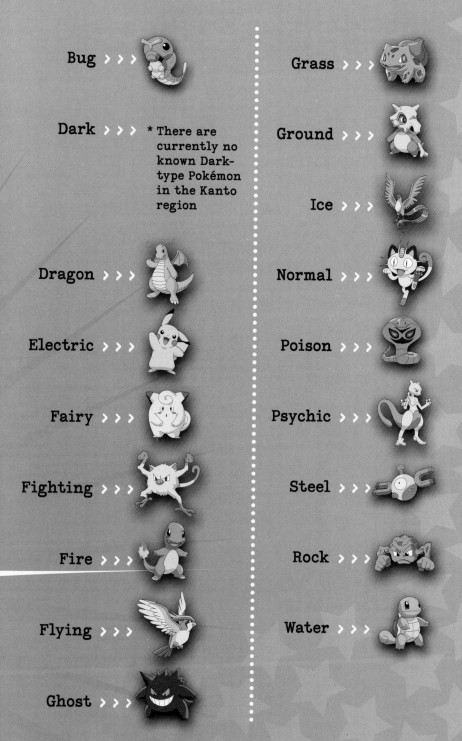

Bug >>>

Grass >>>

Dark >>> *There are
currently no
known Dark-
type Pokémon
in the Kanto
region

Ground >>>

Ice >>>

Dragon >>>

Normal >>>

Electric >>>

Poison >>>

Fairy >>>

Psychic >>>

Fighting >>>

Steel >>>

Fire >>>

Rock >>>

Flying >>>

Water >>>

Ghost >>>

Battle Basics

WHY BATTLE?

There are two basic reasons for a Pokémon to battle. One is for sport. You can battle another Trainer in a friendly competition. Your Pokémon do the fighting, but you decide which Pokémon and which attacks to use.

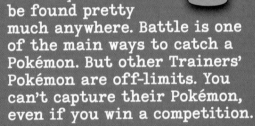

The second reason is to catch wild Pokémon. Wild Pokémon have no training and no owners. They can be found pretty much anywhere. Battle is one of the main ways to catch a Pokémon. But other Trainers' Pokémon are off-limits. You can't capture their Pokémon, even if you win a competition.

Choosing the Best Pokémon for the Job

As you prepare for your first battle, you may have several Pokémon to choose from. Use the resources in this book to help you decide which Pokémon would be best. If you're facing a Fire-type like Charmander, you can quench its heat with a Water-type like Squirtle.

THE FACE-OFF

You and your Pokémon will have to face and hopefully defeat each and every Pokémon on the other Trainer's team. You win when your Pokémon have defeated all the other Trainer's Pokémon. A Pokémon is defeated when it gets so weak it faints.

Ready to discover more about each Pokémon? Then let's begin!

Pokédex Stats and Facts

Bulbasaur

SEED POKÉMON

TYPE: GRASS-POISON

Bulbasaur likes to take a nap in the sunshine. While it sleeps, the seed on its back catches the rays and uses the energy to grow.

HOW TO SAY IT: BUL-ba-sore
IMPERIAL HEIGHT: 2' 04"
METRIC HEIGHT: 0.7m

IMPERIAL WEIGHT: 15.2 lbs.
METRIC WEIGHT: 6.9 kg

POSSIBLE MOVES: Tackle, Growl, Leech Seed, Vine Whip, Poison Powder, Sleep Powder, Take Down, Razor Leaf, Sweet Scent, Growth, Double Edge, Worry Seed, Synthesis, Seed Bomb

EVOLUTION

Bulbasaur › Ivysaur › Venusaur

Ivysaur

SEED POKÉMON

TYPE: GRASS-POISON

Carrying the weight of the bud on its back makes Ivysaur's legs stronger. When the bud is close to blooming, the Pokémon spends more time sleeping in the sun.

HOW TO SAY IT: EYE-vee-sore
IMPERIAL HEIGHT: 3' 03"
METRIC HEIGHT: 1.0m
IMPERIAL WEIGHT: 28.7 lbs.
METRIC WEIGHT: 13.0 kg

POSSIBLE MOVES: Tackle, Growl, Leech Seed, Vine Whip, Poison Powder, Sleep Powder, Take Down, Razor Leaf, Sweet Scent, Growth, Double Edge, Worry Seed, Synthesis, Solar Beam

EVOLUTION

Bulbasaur › Ivysaur › Venusaur

Venusaur

SEED POKÉMON

TYPE: GRASS-POISON

When Venusaur is well nourished and spends enough time in the sun, the flower on its back is brightly colored. The blossom gives off a soothing scent.

HOW TO SAY IT: VEE-nuh-sore
IMPERIAL HEIGHT: 6' 07"
METRIC HEIGHT: 2.0m
IMPERIAL WEIGHT: 220.5 lbs.
METRIC WEIGHT: 100.0 kg

POSSIBLE MOVES: Tackle, Growl, Vine Whip, Leech Seed, Poison Powder, Sleep Powder, Take Down, Razor Leaf, Sweet Scent, Growth, Double Edge, Petal Dance, Worry Seed, Synthesis, Petal Blizzard, Solar Beam

EVOLUTION

Bulbasaur › Ivysaur › Venusaur

#004
Charmander
LIZARD POKÉMON

TYPE: *FIRE*

The flame on Charmander's tail tip indicates how the Pokémon is feeling. It flares up in a fury when Charmander is angry!

HOW TO SAY IT: CHAR-man-der
IMPERIAL HEIGHT: 2' 00"
METRIC HEIGHT: 0.6m
IMPERIAL WEIGHT: 18.7 lbs.
METRIC WEIGHT: 8.5 kg

POSSIBLE MOVES: Scratch, Growl, Ember, Smokescreen, Dragon Rage, Scary Face, Fire Fang, Flame Burst, Slash, Flamethrower, Fire Spin, Inferno

EVOLUTION
Charmander › Charmeleon › Charizard

#005
Charmeleon
FLAME POKÉMON

TYPE: *FIRE*

When Charmeleon takes on a powerful opponent in battle, its tail flame glows white-hot. Its claws are very sharp.

HOW TO SAY IT: char-MEE-lee-un
IMPERIAL HEIGHT: 3' 07"
METRIC HEIGHT: 1.1m
IMPERIAL WEIGHT: 41.9 lbs.
METRIC WEIGHT: 10.0 kg

POSSIBLE MOVES: Scratch, Growl, Ember, Smokescreen, Dragon Rage, Scary Face, Fire Fang, Flame Burst, Slash, Flamethrower, Fire Spin, Inferno

EVOLUTION

Charmander › Charmeleon › Charizard

#006
Charizard
FLAME POKÉMON

TYPE: *FIRE*

Charizard seeks out stronger foes and only breathes fire during battles with worthy opponents. The fiery breath is so hot that it can turn any material to slag.

HOW TO SAY IT: CHAR-iz-ard
IMPERIAL HEIGHT: 5' 07"
METRIC HEIGHT: 1.7m
IMPERIAL WEIGHT: 199.5 lbs.
METRIC WEIGHT: 90.5 kg

POSSIBLE MOVES: Flare Blitz, Heat Wave, Dragon Claw, Shadow Claw, Air Slash, Scratch, Growl, Ember, Smoke-screen, Dragon Rage, Scary Face, Fire Fang, Flame Burst, Wing Attack, Slash, Flamethrower, Fire Spin, Inferno

EVOLUTION

Charmander › Charmeleon › Charizard

#007
Squirtle
TINY TURTLE POKÉMON

TYPE: *WATER*

With its aerodynamic shape and grooved surface, Squirtle's shell helps it cut through the water very quickly. It also offers protection in battle.

HOW TO SAY IT: SKWIR-tul
IMPERIAL HEIGHT: 1' 08"
METRIC HEIGHT: 0.5m

IMPERIAL WEIGHT: 19.8 lbs.
METRIC WEIGHT: 9.0 kg

POSSIBLE MOVES: Tackle, Tail Whip, Water Gun, Withdraw, Bubble, Bite, Rapid Spin, Protect, Water Pulse, Aqua Tail, Skull Bash, Iron Defense, Rain Dance, Hydro Pump

EVOLUTION

Squirtle ▸ Wartortle ▸ Blastoise

(20)

#008
Wartortle
TURTLE POKÉMON

TYPE: *WATER*

The fur on Wartortle's tail darkens with age. Its shell bears the scratches of many battles.

HOW TO SAY IT: WOR-TORE-tul
IMPERIAL HEIGHT: 3' 03"
METRIC HEIGHT: 1.0m
IMPERIAL WEIGHT: 49.6 lbs.
METRIC WEIGHT: 22.5 kg

POSSIBLE MOVES: Tackle, Tail Whip, Water Gun, Withdraw, Bubble, Bite, Rapid Spin, Protect, Water Pulse, Aqua Tail, Skull Bash, Iron Defense, Rain Dance, Hydro Pump

EVOLUTION

Squirtle › Wartortle › Blastoise

Blastoise
#009
SHELLFISH POKÉMON

TYPE: *WATER*

From the spouts on its shell, Blastoise can fire water bullets with amazing accuracy. It can hit a target more than 160 feet away!

HOW TO SAY IT: BLAS-toyce
IMPERIAL HEIGHT: 5' 03"
METRIC HEIGHT: 1.6m
IMPERIAL WEIGHT: 188.5 lbs.
METRIC WEIGHT: 85.5 kg

POSSIBLE MOVES: Flash Cannon, Tackle, Tail Whip, Water Gun, Withdraw, Bubble, Bite, Rapid Spin, Protect, Water Pulse, Aqua Tail, Skull Bash, Iron Defense, Rain Dance, Hydro Pump

EVOLUTION

Squirtle › Wartortle › Blastoise

Caterpie

#010

WORM POKÉMON

TYPE: BUG

A ravenous Caterpie can quickly gobble up leaves that are bigger than itself. Its antenna can produce a terrible smell.

HOW TO SAY IT: CAT-ur-pee
IMPERIAL HEIGHT: 1' 00"
METRIC HEIGHT: 0.3m

IMPERIAL WEIGHT: 6.4 lbs.
METRIC WEIGHT: 2.9 kg

POSSIBLE MOVES: Tackle, String Shot, Bug Bite

EVOLUTION

Caterpie › Metapod › Butterfree

#011

Metapod

COCOON POKÉMON

TYPE: BUG

Inside its iron-hard shell, Metapod patiently prepares to evolve. It doesn't move much, so it relies on its shell for protection.

HOW TO SAY IT: MET-uh-pod
IMPERIAL HEIGHT: 2' 04"
METRIC HEIGHT: 0.7m

IMPERIAL WEIGHT: 21.8 lbs.
METRIC WEIGHT: 9.9 kg

POSSIBLE MOVE: Harden

EVOLUTION

Caterpie › Metapod › Butterfree

#012
Butterfree
BUTTERFLY POKÉMON

TYPE: BUG-FLYING

Butterfree is excellent at seeking out flowers with the most delicious nectar. It sometimes flies more than six miles to locate its favorite food.

HOW TO SAY IT: BUT-er-free

IMPERIAL HEIGHT: 3' 07"
METRIC HEIGHT: 1.1m

IMPERIAL WEIGHT: 70.5 lbs.
METRIC WEIGHT: 32.0 kg

POSSIBLE MOVES: Confusion, Poison Powder, Stun Spore, Sleep Powder, Gust, Supersonic, Whirlwind, Psybeam, Silver Wind, Tailwind, Rage Powder, Safeguard, Captivate, Bug Buzz, Quiver Dance

EVOLUTION

Caterpie › Metapod › Butterfree

(23)

#013 Weedle
HAIRY BUG POKÉMON

TYPE: *BUG-POISON*

Weedle's sense of smell is excellent. With its large red nose, it can sniff out the leaves it likes best.

HOW TO SAY IT: WEE-dull
IMPERIAL HEIGHT: 1' 00"
METRIC HEIGHT: 0.3m

IMPERIAL WEIGHT: 7.1 lbs.
METRIC WEIGHT: 3.2 kg

POSSIBLE MOVES: Poison Sting, String Shot, Bug Bite

EVOLUTION
Weedle › Kakuna › Beedrill

#014 Kakuna
COCOON POKÉMON

TYPE: *BUG-POISON*

Kakuna appears motionless from the outside, but inside its shell, it's busily preparing to evolve. Sometimes the shell heats up from this activity.

HOW TO SAY IT: kah-KOO-na
IMPERIAL HEIGHT: 2' 00"
METRIC HEIGHT: 0.6m

IMPERIAL WEIGHT: 22.0 lbs.
METRIC WEIGHT: 10.0 kg

POSSIBLE MOVE: Harden

EVOLUTION
  Weedle › Kakuna › Beedrill

Beedrill

POISON BEE POKÉMON

TYPE: *BUG-POISON*

Stay far away from a Beedrill nest. These territorial Pokémon will swarm any intruder in a furious attack.

HOW TO SAY IT: BEE-drill

IMPERIAL HEIGHT: 3' 03"
METRIC HEIGHT: 1.0m

IMPERIAL WEIGHT: 65.0 lbs.
METRIC WEIGHT: 29.5 kg

POSSIBLE MOVES: Fury Attack, Focus Energy, Twineedle, Rage, Pursuit, Toxic Spikes, Pin Missile, Agility, Assurance, Poison Jab, Endeavor, Fell Stinger

EVOLUTION

Weedle › Kakuna › Beedrill

#016
Pidgey
TINY BIRD POKÉMON

TYPE: NORMAL-FLYING

Thanks to Pidgey's excellent sense of direction, it can always find its way home, no matter how far it has traveled.

HOW TO SAY IT: PIDG-ee
IMPERIAL HEIGHT: 1' 00"
METRIC HEIGHT: 1.1m

IMPERIAL WEIGHT: 4.0 lbs.
METRIC WEIGHT: 30.0 kg

POSSIBLE MOVES: Tackle, Sand Attack, Gust, Quick Attack, Whirlwind, Twister, Feather Dance, Agility, Wing Attack, Roost, Tailwind, Mirror Move, Air Slash, Hurricane

EVOLUTION

Pidgey › Pidgeotto › Pidgeot

#017
Pidgeotto
BIRD POKÉMON

TYPE: NORMAL-FLYING

Very territorial, Pidgeotto keeps up a steady patrol of the large area it claims as its own. Any intruder will be driven off with merciless attacks from its sharp claws.

HOW TO SAY IT: PIDG-ee-OH-toe
IMPERIAL HEIGHT: 3' 07"
METRIC HEIGHT: 1.1m
IMPERIAL WEIGHT: 66.1 lbs.
METRIC WEIGHT: 30.0 kg

POSSIBLE MOVES: Tackle, Sand Attack, Gust, Quick Attack, Whirlwind, Twister, Feather Dance, Agility, Wing Attack, Roost, Tailwind, Mirror Move, Air Slash, Hurricane

EVOLUTION

Pidgey › Pidgeotto › Pidgeot

#018
Pidgeot
BIRD POKÉMON

TYPE: NORMAL-FLYING

Many Trainers are drawn to Pidgeot because of its lovely feathers. The beautiful colors of its crest are particularly striking.

HOW TO SAY IT: PIDG-ee-ott
IMPERIAL HEIGHT: 4' 11"
METRIC HEIGHT: 1.5m
IMPERIAL WEIGHT: 87.1 lbs.
METRIC WEIGHT: 39.5 kg

POSSIBLE MOVES: Tackle, Sand Attack, Gust, Quick Attack, Whirlwind, Twister, Feather Dance, Agility, Wing Attack, Roost, Tailwind, Mirror Move, Air Slash, Hurricane

Pidgey › Pidgeotto › Pidgeot

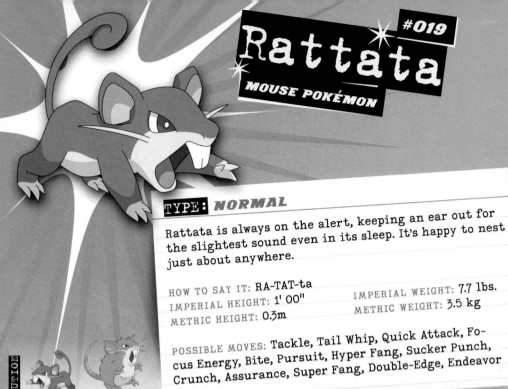

Rattata

#019

MOUSE POKÉMON

TYPE: NORMAL

Rattata is always on the alert, keeping an ear out for the slightest sound even in its sleep. It's happy to nest just about anywhere.

HOW TO SAY IT: RA-TAT-ta
IMPERIAL HEIGHT: 1' 00"
METRIC HEIGHT: 0.3m
IMPERIAL WEIGHT: 7.7 lbs.
METRIC WEIGHT: 3.5 kg

POSSIBLE MOVES: Tackle, Tail Whip, Quick Attack, Focus Energy, Bite, Pursuit, Hyper Fang, Sucker Punch, Crunch, Assurance, Super Fang, Double-Edge, Endeavor

EVOLUTION
Rattata › Raticate

#020

Raticate

MOUSE POKÉMON

TYPE: NORMAL

Because Raticate's fangs never stop growing, it has to gnaw on hard objects to whittle them down. Logs and rocks often serve this purpose, but sometimes it chews on houses!

HOW TO SAY IT: RAT-ih-kate
IMPERIAL HEIGHT: 2' 04"
METRIC HEIGHT: 0.7m
IMPERIAL WEIGHT: 40.8 lbs.
METRIC WEIGHT: 18.5 kg

POSSIBLE MOVES: Swords Dance, Tackle, Tail Whip, Quick Attack, Focus Energy, Bite, Pursuit, Hyper Fang, Sucker Punch, Crunch, Assurance, Super Fang, Double-Edge, Endeavor

EVOLUTION

Rattata › Raticate

#021

Spearow

TINY BIRD POKÉMON

TYPE: *NORMAL-FLYING*

When many Spearow sound their loud, high-pitched cry all at once, it usually means danger is nearby.

HOW TO SAY IT: SPEA-row
IMPERIAL HEIGHT: 1' 00"
METRIC HEIGHT: 0.3m

IMPERIAL WEIGHT: 4.4 lbs.
METRIC WEIGHT: 2.0 kg

POSSIBLE MOVES: Peck, Growl, Leer, Fury Attack, Pursuit, Aerial Ace, Mirror Move, Agility, Assurance, Roost, Drill Peck

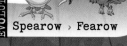

Spearow › Fearow

#022

Fearow

BEAK POKÉMON

TYPE: *NORMAL-FLYING*

Fearow's long, thin beak is the perfect tool for digging up food from the dirt or catching it in the water.

HOW TO SAY IT: FEER-ow
IMPERIAL HEIGHT: 3' 11"
METRIC HEIGHT: 1.2m

IMPERIAL WEIGHT: 83.8 lbs.
METRIC WEIGHT: 38.0 kg

POSSIBLE MOVES: Drill Run, Pluck, Peck, Growl, Leer, Fury Attack, Pursuit, Aerial Ace, Mirror Move, Agility, Assurance, Roost, Drill Peck

Spearow › Fearow

(29)

#023 Ekans
SNAKE POKÉMON

TYPE: *POISON*

When Ekans rests, it coils its long body up into a spiral. In this position, it can quickly raise its head to challenge a foe.

HOW TO SAY IT: ECK-kins
IMPERIAL HEIGHT: 6' 07"
METRIC HEIGHT: 2.0m

IMPERIAL WEIGHT: 15.2 lbs.
METRIC WEIGHT: 6.9 kg

POSSIBLE MOVES: Wrap, Leer, Poison Sting, Bite, Glare, Screech, Acid, Stockpile, Swallow, Spit Up, Acid Spray, Mud Bomb, Gastro Acid, Belch, Haze, Coil, Gunk Shot

EVOLUTION
Ekans › Arbok

#024
Arbok
COBRA POKÉMON

TYPE: *POISON*

A powerful constrictor, Arbok can crush a steel barrel in its mighty coils. Getting out of its grip is no small feat.

HOW TO SAY IT: ARE-bock
IMPERIAL HEIGHT: 11' 06"
METRIC HEIGHT: 3.5m

IMPERIAL WEIGHT: 143.3 lbs.
METRIC WEIGHT: 65.0 kg

POSSIBLE MOVES: Ice Fang, Thunder Fang, Fire Fang, Wrap, Leer, Poison Sting, Bite, Glare, Screech, Acid, Crunch, Stockpile, Swallow, Spit Up, Acid Spray, Mud Bomb, Gastro Acid, Belch, Haze, Coil, Gunk Shot

EVOLUTION
Ekans › Arbok

#025
Pikachu
MOUSE POKÉMON

TYPE: *ELECTRIC*

The red pouches on Pikachu's cheeks store up electricity while it sleeps. It often delivers a zap when encountering something unfamiliar.

HOW TO SAY IT: PEE-ka-choo
IMPERIAL HEIGHT: 1' 04"
METRIC HEIGHT: 0.4m

IMPERIAL WEIGHT: 13.2 lbs.
METRIC WEIGHT: 6.0 kg

POSSIBLE MOVES: Tail Whip, Thunder Shock, Growl, Play Nice, Quick Attack, Thunder Wave, Electro Ball, Double Team, Nuzzle, Slam, Thunderbolt, Feint, Agility, Discharge, Light Screen, Thunder

EVOLUTION

Pikachu › Raichu

#026
Raichu
MOUSE POKÉMON

TYPE: *ELECTRIC*

When overcharged with electricity, Raichu sinks its tail into the ground to get rid of the excess. The charge makes it glow faintly in the dark.

HOW TO SAY IT: RYE-choo
IMPERIAL HEIGHT: 2' 0"
METRIC HEIGHT: 0.8m

IMPERIAL WEIGHT: 66.1 lbs.
METRIC WEIGHT: 30.0 kg

POSSIBLE MOVES: Thunder Shock, Tail Whip, Quick Attack, Thunderbolt

EVOLUTION

Pikachu › Raichu

Sandshrew

#027

MOUSE POKÉMON

TYPE: *GROUND*

When Sandshrew rolls up into a ball, its tough hide helps keep it safe. It lives in the desert and sleeps in a burrow under the sand.

HOW TO SAY IT: **SAND-shroo**
IMPERIAL HEIGHT: 2' 00"
METRIC HEIGHT: 0.6m

IMPERIAL WEIGHT: 26.5 lbs.
METRIC WEIGHT: 12.0 kg

POSSIBLE MOVES: Scratch, Defense Curl, Sand Attack, Poison Sting, Rollout, Rapid Spin, Swift, Fury Cutter, Magnitude, Fury Swipes, Sand Tomb, Slash, Dig, Gyro Ball, Swords Dance, Sandstorm, Earthquake

EVOLUTION

Sandshrew › Sandslash

Sandslash

#028

MOUSE POKÉMON

TYPE: *GROUND*

Sections of hardened hide form the spikes that cover Sandslash's body. The spikes protect it in battle and can also be used as a weapon.

HOW TO SAY IT: **SAND-slash**
IMPERIAL HEIGHT: 3' 03"
METRIC HEIGHT: 1.0m

IMPERIAL WEIGHT: 65.0 lbs.
METRIC WEIGHT: 29.5 kg

POSSIBLE MOVES: Scratch, Defense Curl, Sand Attack, Poison Sting, Rollout, Rapid Spin, Swift, Fury Cutter, Magnitude, Fury Swipes, Crush Claw, Sand Tomb, Slash, Dig, Gyro Ball, Swords Dance, Sandstorm, Earthquake

EVOLUTION

Sandshrew › Sandslash

Nidoran♀

POISON PIN POKÉMON

TYPE: POISON

Though Nidoran ♀ is small, it's quite dangerous. The barbs in its fur and the horn on its head are both extremely poisonous.

HOW TO SAY IT: NEE-doe-ran
IMPERIAL HEIGHT: 1' 04"
METRIC HEIGHT: 0.4m

IMPERIAL WEIGHT: 15.4 lbs.
METRIC WEIGHT: 7.0 kg

POSSIBLE MOVES: Growl, Scratch, Tail Whip, Double Kick, Poison Sting, Fury Swipes, Bite, Helping Hand, Toxic Spikes, Flatter, Crunch, Captivate, Poison Fang

EVOLUTION Nidoran ♀ › Nidorina › Nidoqueen

#030
Nidorina
POISON PIN POKÉMON

TYPE: *POISON*

Nidorina are very social and become nervous on their own. When among friends, their poisonous barbs retract so they don't hurt anyone.

HOW TO SAY IT: NEE-doe-REE-na
IMPERIAL HEIGHT: 2' 07"
METRIC HEIGHT: 0.8m

IMPERIAL WEIGHT: 44.1 lbs.
METRIC WEIGHT: 20.0 kg

POSSIBLE MOVES: Growl, Scratch, Tail Whip, Double Kick, Poison Sting, Fury Swipes, Bite, Helping Hand, Toxic Spikes, Flatter, Crunch, Captivate, Poison Fang

EVOLUTION
Nidoran › Nidorina › Nidoqueen

#031
Nidoqueen
DRILL POKÉMON

TYPE: *POISON-GROUND*

When defending its nest, Nidoqueen hurls its hard-scaled body at an intruder. The impact is often enough to send the enemy flying through the air.

HOW TO SAY IT: NEE-doe-kween
IMPERIAL HEIGHT: 4' 03"
METRIC HEIGHT: 1.3m

IMPERIAL WEIGHT: 132.3 lbs.
METRIC WEIGHT: 60.0 kg

POSSIBLE MOVES: Superpower, Scratch, Tail Whip, Double Kick, Poison Sting, Chip Away, Body Slam, Earth Power

EVOLUTION
Nidoran ♀ › Nidorina › Nidoqueen

#032
Nidoran♂
POISON PIN POKÉMON

TYPE: *POISON*

Nidoran ♂ has excellent hearing and, thanks to specialized muscles, it can move and rotate its ears to pick up the slightest sound.

HOW TO SAY IT: NEE-doe-ran
IMPERIAL HEIGHT: 1' 08"
METRIC HEIGHT: 0.5m

IMPERIAL WEIGHT: 19.8 lbs.
METRIC WEIGHT: 9.0 kg

POSSIBLE MOVES: Leer, Peck, Focus Energy, Double Kick, Poison Sting, Fury Attack, Horn Attack, Helping Hand, Toxic Spikes, Flatter, Poison Jab, Captivate, Horn Drill

EVOLUTION

Nidoran ♂ › Nidorino › Nidoking

#033 Nidorino

POISON PIN POKÉMON

TYPE: *POISON*

The horn on Nidorino's forehead is made of an extremely hard substance. When challenged, its body bristles with poisonous barbs.

HOW TO SAY IT: NEE-doe-REE-no
IMPERIAL HEIGHT: 2' 11"
METRIC HEIGHT: 0.9m

IMPERIAL WEIGHT: 43.0 lbs.
METRIC WEIGHT: 19.5 kg

POSSIBLE MOVES: Leer, Peck, Focus Energy, Double Kick, Poison Sting, Fury Attack, Horn Attack, Helping Hand, Toxic Spikes, Flatter, Poison Jab, Captivate, Horn Drill

EVOLUTION

Nidoran ♂ › Nidorino › Nidoking

#034 Nidoking

DRILL POKÉMON

TYPE: *POISON-GROUND*

When Nidoking swings its massive tail, it can knock down a radio tower. Nothing can stand in the way of its furious rampage.

HOW TO SAY IT: NEE-doe-king
IMPERIAL HEIGHT: 4' 07"
METRIC HEIGHT: 1.4m

IMPERIAL WEIGHT: 136.7 lbs.
METRIC WEIGHT: 62.0 kg

POSSIBLE MOVES: Megahorn, Peck, Focus Energy, Double Kick, Poison Sting, Chip Away, Thrash, Earth Power

EVOLUTION

Nidoran ♂ › Nidorino › Nidoking

Clefairy #035

FAIRY POKÉMON

TYPE: *FAIRY*

Groups of Clefairy gather to play under the full moon. When the sun rises, they retreat to their mountain home and snuggle together to sleep.

HOW TO SAY IT: kleh-FAIR-ee
IMPERIAL HEIGHT: 2' 00"
METRIC HEIGHT: 0.6m
IMPERIAL WEIGHT: 16.5 lbs.
METRIC WEIGHT: 7.5 kg

POSSIBLE MOVES: Pound, Growl, Encore, Sing, Double Slap, Defense Curl, Follow Me, Minimize, Wake-Up Slap, Bestow, Cosmic Power, Lucky Chant, Metronome, Gravity, Moonlight, Stored Power, Light Screen, Healing Wish, After You

EVOLUTION
Clefairy › Clefable

#036 Clefable

FAIRY POKÉMON

TYPE: *FAIRY*

Clefable moves with such lightness that it can skip across the water—perfect for a moonlight stroll on the surface of a lake.

HOW TO SAY IT: kleh-FAY-bull
IMPERIAL HEIGHT: 4' 03"
METRIC HEIGHT: 1.3m
IMPERIAL WEIGHT: 88.2 lbs.
METRIC WEIGHT: 40.0 kg

POSSIBLE MOVES: Sing, Double Slap, Minimize, Metronome

EVOLUTION

Clefairy › Clefable

#037
Vulpix
FOX POKÉMON

TYPE: *FIRE*

Vulpix starts its life with a single tail that splits into six as it grows. The fire inside its body is constantly burning.

HOW TO SAY IT: VULL-picks
IMPERIAL HEIGHT: 2' 00"
METRIC HEIGHT: 0.6m
IMPERIAL WEIGHT: 21.8 lbs.
METRIC WEIGHT: 9.9 kg

POSSIBLE MOVES: Ember, Tail Whip, Roar, Quick Attack, Fire Spin, Confuse Ray, Imprison, Flame Burst, Safeguard, Will-O-Wisp, Payback, Flamethrower, Captivate, Inferno, Grudge, Extrasensory, Fire Blast

EVOLUTION

Vulpix › Ninetales

Ninetales
#038
FOX POKÉMON

TYPE: *FIRE*

Ninetales can control an opponent's mind with the light from its red eyes. Stories say this Pokémon was formed when nine wizards merged into a single being.

HOW TO SAY IT: NINE-tails
IMPERIAL HEIGHT: 3' 07"
METRIC HEIGHT: 1.1m
IMPERIAL WEIGHT: 43.9 lbs.
METRIC WEIGHT: 19.9 kg

POSSIBLE MOVES: Nasty Plot, Ember, Quick Attack, Confuse Ray, Safeguard

EVOLUTION

Vulpix › Ninetales

#039
Jigglypuff
BALLOON POKÉMON

TYPE: *NORMAL-FAIRY*

Jigglypuff's primary weapon is its song, which lulls opponents to sleep. Because it never stops to breathe while singing, long battles can put it in danger.

HOW TO SAY IT: JIG-lee-puff
IMPERIAL HEIGHT: 1' 08"
METRIC HEIGHT: 0.5m

IMPERIAL WEIGHT: 12.1 lbs.
METRIC WEIGHT: 5.5 kg

POSSIBLE MOVES: Sing, Defense Curl, Pound, Play Nice, Disable, Round, Rollout, Double Slap, Rest, Body Slam, Gyro Ball, Wake-Up Slap, Mimic, Hyper Voice, Disarming Voice, Double-Edge

EVOLUTION

Jigglypuff › Wigglytuff

Wigglytuff

BALLOON POKÉMON

TYPE: NORMAL-FAIRY

A protective coating of tears covers Wigglytuff's enormous eyes, keeping the dust away. It can suck in air to inflate its flexible body until it resembles a balloon.

HOW TO SAY IT: WIG-lee-tuff
IMPERIAL HEIGHT: 3' 03"
METRIC HEIGHT: 1.0m

IMPERIAL WEIGHT: 26.5 lbs.
METRIC WEIGHT: 12.0 kg

POSSIBLE MOVES: Double-Edge, Play Rough, Sing, Disable, Defense Curl, Double Slap

EVOLUTION

Jigglypuff › Wigglytuff

(41)

TYPE: *POISON-FLYING*

Sunlight isn't good for Zubat, so it stays hidden during the day. It prefers dark places like caves and old houses.

HOW TO SAY IT: ZOO-bat
IMPERIAL HEIGHT: 2' 07"
METRIC HEIGHT: 0.8m

IMPERIAL WEIGHT: 16.5 lbs.
METRIC WEIGHT: 7.5 kg

POSSIBLE MOVES: Leech Life, Supersonic, Astonish, Bite, Wing Attack, Confuse Ray, Swift, Air Cutter, Acrobatics, Mean Look, Poison Fang, Haze, Air Slash

EVOLUTION
Zubat › Golbat

#042
Golbat
BAT POKÉMON

TYPE: *POISON-FLYING*

With its four sharp fangs, Golbat feeds on living beings. Darkness gives it an advantage in battle, and it prefers to attack on pitch-black nights.

HOW TO SAY IT: GOL-bat
IMPERIAL HEIGHT: 5' 03"
METRIC HEIGHT: 1.6m

IMPERIAL WEIGHT: 121.3 lbs.
METRIC WEIGHT: 55.0 kg

POSSIBLE MOVES: Screech, Leech Life, Supersonic, Astonish, Bite, Wing Attack, Confuse Ray, Swift, Air Cutter, Acrobatics, Mean Look, Poison Fang, Haze, Air Slash

EVOLUTION
Zubat › Golbat

Oddish

WEED POKÉMON

TYPE: *GRASS-POISON*

Oddish seeks out fertile ground where it can absorb nutrients from the soil. When it finds the perfect spot, it buries itself, and its feet apparently become like tree roots.

HOW TO SAY IT: ODD-ish
IMPERIAL HEIGHT: 1' 08"
METRIC HEIGHT: 0.5m

IMPERIAL WEIGHT: 11.9 lbs.
METRIC WEIGHT: 5.4 kg

POSSIBLE MOVES: Absorb, Sweet Scent, Acid, Poison Powder, Stun Spore, Sleep Powder, Mega Drain, Lucky Chant, Natural Gift, Moonlight, Giga Drain, Petal Dance, Grassy Terrain

EVOLUTION

Oddish › Gloom › Vileplume

Gloom
WEED POKÉMON

TYPE: *GRASS-POISON*

Gloom doesn't always smell terrible—when it feels safe and relaxed, its aroma fades. However, its nectar usually carries an awful stench.

HOW TO SAY IT: GLOOM
IMPERIAL HEIGHT: 2' 07"
METRIC HEIGHT: 0.8m

IMPERIAL WEIGHT: 19.0 lbs.
METRIC WEIGHT: 8.6 kg

POSSIBLE MOVES: Absorb, Sweet Scent, Acid, Poison Powder, Stun Spore, Sleep Powder, Mega Drain, Lucky Chant, Natural Gift, Moonlight, Giga Drain, Petal Blizzard, Petal Dance, Grassy Terrain

EVOLUTION

Oddish › Gloom › Vileplume

Vileplume
FLOWER POKÉMON

TYPE: *GRASS-POISON*

Many people are terribly allergic to the poisonous pollen Vileplume gives off. The petals of its flower are truly enormous.

HOW TO SAY IT: VILE-ploom
IMPERIAL HEIGHT: 3' 11"
METRIC HEIGHT: 1.2m

IMPERIAL WEIGHT: 41.0 lbs.
METRIC WEIGHT: 18.6 kg

POSSIBLE MOVES: Mega Drain, Aromatherapy, Stun Spore, Poison Powder, Petal Blizzard, Petal Dance, Solar Beam

EVOLUTION

Oddish › Gloom › Vileplume

#046 Paras

MUSHROOM POKÉMON

TYPE: *BUG-GRASS*

Mushrooms called tochukaso grow on Paras's back. Some people use them in medicines.

HOW TO SAY IT: PARE-iss
IMPERIAL HEIGHT: 1' 00"
METRIC HEIGHT: 0.3m
IMPERIAL WEIGHT: 11.9 lbs.
METRIC WEIGHT: 5.4 kg

POSSIBLE MOVES: Scratch, Stun Spore, Poison Powder, Leech Life, Fury Cutter, Spore, Slash, Growth, Giga Drain, Aromatherapy, Rage Powder, X-Scissor

EVOLUTION

Paras › Parasect

#047 Parasect

MUSHROOM POKÉMON

TYPE: *BUG-GRASS*

Parasect feed on the roots of trees. If a group of them infests the same tree, they can be very destructive.

HOW TO SAY IT: PARE-a-sekt
IMPERIAL HEIGHT: 3' 03"
METRIC HEIGHT: 1.0m
IMPERIAL WEIGHT: 65.0 lbs.
METRIC WEIGHT: 29.5 kg

POSSIBLE MOVES: Cross Poison, Scratch, Stun Spore, Poison Powder, Leech Life, Fury Cutter, Spore, Slash, Growth, Giga Drain, Aromatherapy, Rage Powder, X-Scissor

EVOLUTION

Paras › Parasect

Venonat #048

INSECT POKÉMON

TYPE: BUG-POISON

Venonat's large, sensitive eyes pick up even the tiniest movement. The stiff hair that covers its body protects it from harm.

HOW TO SAY IT: VEH-no-nat
IMPERIAL HEIGHT: 3' 03"
METRIC HEIGHT: 1.0m

IMPERIAL WEIGHT: 66.1 lbs.
METRIC WEIGHT: 30.0 kg

POSSIBLE MOVES: Tackle, Disable, Foresight, Supersonic, Confusion, Poison Powder, Leech Life, Stun Spore, Psybeam, Sleep Powder, Signal Beam, Zen Headbutt, Poison Fang, Psychic

EVOLUTION
Venonat › Venomoth

#049 Venomoth

POISON MOTH POKÉMON

TYPE: BUG-POISON

When they become active after dark, Venomoth are often drawn to street lamps. It isn't the light that attracts them, but the promise of food.

HOW TO SAY IT: VEH-no-moth
IMPERIAL HEIGHT: 4' 11"
METRIC HEIGHT: 1.5m

IMPERIAL WEIGHT: 27.6 lbs.
METRIC WEIGHT: 12.5 kg

POSSIBLE MOVES: Silver Wind, Tackle, Disable, Foresight, Supersonic, Confusion, Poison Powder, Leech Life, Stun Spore, Psybeam, Sleep Powder, Gust, Signal Beam, Zen Headbutt, Poison Fang, Psychic, Bug Buzz, Quiver Dance

EVOLUTION
Venonat › Venomoth

#050 Diglett

MOLE POKÉMON

TYPE: GROUND

Farmers love having Diglett around. As these Pokémon burrow through the ground, they leave the soil in perfect condition for planting.

HOW TO SAY IT: DIG-let
IMPERIAL HEIGHT: 0' 08"
METRIC HEIGHT: 0.2m

IMPERIAL WEIGHT: 1.8 lbs.
METRIC WEIGHT: 0.8 kg

POSSIBLE MOVES: Scratch, Sand Attack, Growl, Astonish, Mud-Slap, Magnitude, Bulldoze, Sucker Punch, Mud Bomb, Earth Power, Dig, Slash, Earthquake, Fissure

EVOLUTION

Diglett › Dugtrio

#051 Dugtrio

MOLE POKÉMON

TYPE: GROUND

When it comes to digging, Dugtrio knows that three heads are better than one. The triplets think alike and work together.

HOW TO SAY IT: DUG-TREE-oh
IMPERIAL HEIGHT: 2' 04"
METRIC HEIGHT: 0.7m

IMPERIAL WEIGHT: 73.4 lbs.
METRIC WEIGHT: 33.3 kg

POSSIBLE MOVES: Rototiller, Night Slash, Tri Attack, Scratch, Sand Attack, Growl, Astonish, Mud-Slap, Magnitude, Bulldoze, Sucker Punch, Sand Tomb, Mud Bomb, Earth Power, Dig, Slash, Earthquake, Fissure

EVOLUTION

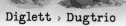

Diglett › Dugtrio

#052

Meowth

SCRATCH CAT POKÉMON

TYPE: NORMAL

When Meowth retracts its sharp claws, it can move without making a sound or leaving a footprint. It's drawn to shiny things like coins.

HOW TO SAY IT: mee-OWTH
IMPERIAL HEIGHT: 1' 04"
METRIC HEIGHT: 0.4m

IMPERIAL WEIGHT: 9.3 lbs.
METRIC WEIGHT: 4.2 kg

POSSIBLE MOVES: Scratch, Growl, Bite, Fake Out, Fury Swipes, Screech, Feint Attack, Taunt, Pay Day, Slash, Nasty Plot, Assurance, Captivate, Night Slash, Feint

EVOLUTION

Meowth › Persian

#053

Persian

CLASSY CAT POKÉMON

TYPE: NORMAL

Persian uses its distinctive whiskers as sensors to find out about its surroundings. Grabbing the whiskers makes it meek and docile.

HOW TO SAY IT: PER-zhun
IMPERIAL HEIGHT: 3' 03"
METRIC HEIGHT: 1.0m

IMPERIAL WEIGHT: 70.5 lbs.
METRIC WEIGHT: 32.0 kg

POSSIBLE MOVES: Switcheroo, Scratch, Growl, Bite, Fake Out, Fury Swipes, Screech, Feint Attack, Taunt, Power Gem, Slash, Nasty Plot, Assurance, Captivate, Night Slash, Feint

EVOLUTION

Meowth › Persian

#054
Psyduck
DUCK POKÉMON

TYPE: *WATER*

Though Psyduck can use mysterious psychic powers, it can never remember doing so. Apparently, this power creates strange brain waves that resemble deep slumber.

HOW TO SAY IT: SY-duck
IMPERIAL HEIGHT: 2' 07"
METRIC HEIGHT: 0.8m

IMPERIAL WEIGHT: 43.2 lbs.
METRIC WEIGHT: 19.6 kg

POSSIBLE MOVES: Water Sport, Scratch, Tail Whip, Water Gun, Disable, Confusion, Water Pulse, Fury Swipes, Screech, Zen Headbutt, Aqua Tail, Soak, Psych Up, Amnesia, Hydro Pump, Wonder Room

EVOLUTION

Psyduck › Golduck

#055

Golduck

DUCK POKÉMON

TYPE: *WATER*

The webbing on its legs makes Golduck an excellent swimmer. Even when facing strong currents and towering waves, it can cut through the water to rescue shipwreck victims.

HOW TO SAY IT: GOL-duck
IMPERIAL HEIGHT: 5' 07"
METRIC HEIGHT: 1.7m

IMPERIAL WEIGHT: 168.9 lbs.
METRIC WEIGHT: 76.6 kg

POSSIBLE MOVES: Aqua Jet, Water Sport, Scratch, Tail Whip, Water Gun, Disable, Confusion, Water Pulse, Fury Swipes, Screech, Zen Headbutt, Aqua Tail, Soak, Psych Up, Amnesia, Hydro Pump, Wonder Room

EVOLUTION

Psyduck › Golduck

(51)

Mankey #056
PIG MONKEY POKÉMON

TYPE: FIGHTING

Mankey flies into a rage at the slightest provocation. These fits of temper are usually preceded by violent tremors, but there's rarely enough time to get away.

HOW TO SAY IT: MAN-key
IMPERIAL HEIGHT: 1' 08"
METRIC HEIGHT: 0.5m

IMPERIAL WEIGHT: 61.7 lbs.
METRIC WEIGHT: 28.0 kg

POSSIBLE MOVES: Covet, Scratch, Low Kick, Leer, Focus Energy, Fury Swipes, Karate Chop, Seismic Toss, Screech, Assurance, Swagger, Cross Chop, Thrash, Punishment, Close Combat, Final Gambit

EVOLUTION

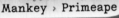

Mankey › Primeape

#057
Primeape
PIG MONKEY POKÉMON

TYPE: FIGHTING

Fury increases Primeape's blood flow and powers up its muscles. Its intelligence drops sharply during a rage.

HOW TO SAY IT: PRIME-ape
IMPERIAL HEIGHT: 3' 03"
METRIC HEIGHT: 1.0m

IMPERIAL WEIGHT: 70.5 lbs.
METRIC WEIGHT: 32.0 kg

POSSIBLE MOVES: Fling, Scratch, Low Kick, Leer, Focus Energy, Fury Swipes, Karate Chop, Seismic Toss, Screech, Assurance, Rage, Swagger, Cross Chop, Thrash, Punishment, Close Combat, Final Gambit

EVOLUTION

Mankey › Primeape

#058
Growlithe
PUPPY POKÉMON

TYPE: *FIRE*

Growlithe has an excellent nose and a good memory for scents. It can even sniff out people's emotions.

HOW TO SAY IT: GROWL-lith
IMPERIAL HEIGHT: 2' 04"
METRIC HEIGHT: 0.7m

IMPERIAL WEIGHT: 41.9 lbs.
METRIC WEIGHT: 19.0 kg

POSSIBLE MOVES: Bite, Roar, Ember, Leer, Odor Sleuth, Helping Hand, Flame Wheel, Reversal, Fire Fang, Flame Burst, Take Down, Flamethrower, Agility, Crunch, Retaliate, Heat Wave, Flare Blitz

EVOLUTION

Growlithe › Arcanine

#059
Arcanine
LEGENDARY POKÉMON

TYPE: *FIRE*

Arcanine's internal flame is the fuel for its amazing speed and endurance. If it runs for a whole day, it can cover more than 6,000 miles.

HOW TO SAY IT: ARE-ka-nine
IMPERIAL HEIGHT: 6' 03"
METRIC HEIGHT: 1.9m

IMPERIAL WEIGHT: 341.7 lbs.
METRIC WEIGHT: 155.0 kg

POSSIBLE MOVES: Thunder Fang, Bite, Roar, Fire Fang, Odor Sleuth, Extreme Speed

EVOLUTION

Growlithe › Arcanine

(53)

#060
Poliwag
TADPOLE POKÉMON

TYPE: WATER

Poliwag's skin is so thin that you can see right through it to the Pokémon's spiral-shaped insides. Fortunately, it's also very resilient and flexible.

HOW TO SAY IT: PAUL-lee-wag
IMPERIAL HEIGHT: 2' 00"
METRIC HEIGHT: 0.6m

IMPERIAL WEIGHT: 27.3 lbs.
METRIC WEIGHT: 12.4 kg

POSSIBLE MOVES: Water Sport, Water Gun, Hypnosis, Bubble, Double Slap, Rain Dance, Body Slam, Bubble Beam, Mud Shot, Belly Drum, Wake-Up Slap, Hydro Pump, Mud Bomb

EVOLUTION

Poliwag › Poliwhirl › Poliwrath

Poliwhirl

TADPOLE POKÉMON

TYPE: WATER

Poliwhirl is covered with a slick, slippery, slimy fluid that allows it to wriggle out of sticky situations.

HOW TO SAY IT: PAUL-lee-wirl
IMPERIAL HEIGHT: 3' 03"
METRIC HEIGHT: 1.0m
IMPERIAL WEIGHT: 44.1 lbs.
METRIC WEIGHT: 20.0 kg

POSSIBLE MOVES: Water Sport, Water Gun, Hypnosis, Bubble, Double Slap, Rain Dance, Body Slam, Bubble Beam, Mud Shot, Belly Drum, Wake-Up Slap, Hydro Pump, Mud Bomb

EVOLUTION

Poliwag › Poliwhirl › Poliwrath

Poliwrath

TADPOLE POKÉMON

TYPE: WATER

Burly and muscular, Poliwrath can exercise for hours without getting tired. It swims effortlessly through the ocean.

HOW TO SAY IT: PAUL-lee-rath
IMPERIAL HEIGHT: 4' 03"
METRIC HEIGHT: 1.3m
IMPERIAL WEIGHT: 119.0 lbs.
METRIC WEIGHT: 54.0 kg

POSSIBLE MOVES: Circle Throw, Bubble Beam, Hypnosis, Double Slap, Submission, Dynamic Punch, Mind Reader

EVOLUTION

Poliwag › Poliwhirl › Poliwrath

#063

Abra

PSI POKÉMON

TYPE: PSYCHIC

Even while Abra is sleeping, which is most of the time, it can escape a foe by teleporting away. If it doesn't get enough sleep, its powers fade.

HOW TO SAY IT: AH-bra
IMPERIAL HEIGHT: 2' 11"
METRIC HEIGHT: 0.9m

IMPERIAL WEIGHT: 43.0 lbs.
METRIC WEIGHT: 19.5 kg

POSSIBLE MOVE: Teleport

EVOLUTION

Abra　›　Kadabra　›　Alakazam

#064
Kadabra
PSI POKÉMON

TYPE: *PSYCHIC*

The silver spoon Kadabra carries intensifies its brain waves. Only those with strong minds should attempt to train this Pokémon.

HOW TO SAY IT: kuh-DAH-bra
IMPERIAL HEIGHT: 4' 03"
METRIC HEIGHT: 1.3m
IMPERIAL WEIGHT: 124.6 lbs.
METRIC WEIGHT: 56.5 kg

POSSIBLE MOVES: Teleport, Kinesis, Confusion, Disable, Miracle Eye, Ally Switch, Psybeam, Reflect, Telekinesis, Recover, Psycho Cut, Role Play, Psychic, Future Sight, Trick

EVOLUTION

Abra › Kadabra › Alakazam

#065
Alakazam
PSI POKÉMON

TYPE: *PSYCHIC*

Because its brain never stops growing, Alakazam must use telekinesis to hold up its heavy head. On the plus side, its memory and intellect are amazing.

HOW TO SAY IT: AH-la-kuh-ZAM
IMPERIAL HEIGHT: 4' 11"
METRIC HEIGHT: 1.5m
IMPERIAL WEIGHT: 105.8 lbs.
METRIC WEIGHT: 48.0 kg

POSSIBLE MOVES: Teleport, Kinesis, Confusion, Disable, Miracle Eye, Ally Switch, Psybeam, Reflect, Telekinesis, Recover, Psycho Cut, Calm Mind, Psychic, Future Sight, Trick

EVOLUTION

Abra › Kadabra › Alakazam

Machop

SUPERPOWER POKÉMON

TYPE: *FIGHTING*

Machop lifts a Graveler like a weight to make its muscles stronger. No matter how much it exercises, it never gets sore.

HOW TO SAY IT: muh-CHOP
IMPERIAL HEIGHT: 2' 07"
METRIC HEIGHT: 0.8m

IMPERIAL WEIGHT: 43.0 lbs.
METRIC WEIGHT: 19.5 kg

POSSIBLE MOVES: Low Kick, Leer, Focus Energy, Karate Chop, Low Sweep, Foresight, Seismic Toss, Revenge, Vital Throw, Submission, Wake-Up Slap, Cross Chop, Scary Face, Dynamic Punch

EVOLUTION
Machop › Machoke › Machamp

#067

Machoke

SUPERPOWER POKÉMON

TYPE: *FIGHTING*

Machoke never stop training. Even when they have jobs helping people with heavy labor, they spend their free time building up their muscles.

HOW TO SAY IT: muh-CHOKE
IMPERIAL HEIGHT: 4' 11"
METRIC HEIGHT: 1.5m

IMPERIAL WEIGHT: 155.4 lbs.
METRIC WEIGHT: 70.5 kg

POSSIBLE MOVES: Low Kick, Leer, Focus Energy, Karate Chop, Low Sweep, Foresight, Seismic Toss, Revenge, Vital Throw, Submission, Wake-Up Slap, Cross Chop, Scary Face, Dynamic Punch

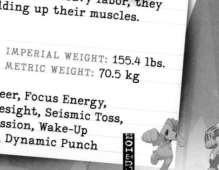

EVOLUTION
Machop › Machoke › Machamp

#068
Machamp
SUPERPOWER POKÉMON

TYPE: *FIGHTING*

Though it is a master of martial arts, Machamp some-times gets its four arms tangled up when trying to do more intricate tasks.

HOW TO SAY IT: muh-CHAMP

IMPERIAL HEIGHT: 5' 03"
METRIC HEIGHT: 1.6m

IMPERIAL WEIGHT: 286.6 lbs.
METRIC WEIGHT: 130.0 kg

POSSIBLE MOVES: Wide Guard, Low Kick, Leer, Focus Energy, Karate Chop, Low Sweep, Foresight, Seismic Toss, Revenge, Vital Throw, Submission, Wake-Up Slap, Cross Chop, Scary Face, Dynamic Punch

Machop › Machoke › Machamp

Bellsprout

FLOWER POKÉMON

TYPE: *GRASS-POISON*

Bellsprout's long, thin body can bend in any direction, so it's good at dodging attacks. The liquid it spits is highly corrosive.

HOW TO SAY IT: BELL-sprout

IMPERIAL HEIGHT: 2' 04"

METRIC HEIGHT: 0.7m

IMPERIAL WEIGHT: 8.8 lbs.

METRIC WEIGHT: 4.0 kg

POSSIBLE MOVES: Vine Whip, Growth, Wrap, Sleep Powder, Poison Powder, Stun Spore, Acid, Knock Off, Sweet Scent, Gastro Acid, Razor Leaf, Slam, Wring Out

EVOLUTION

Bellsprout › Weepinbell › Victreebel

Weepinbell

FLYCATCHER POKÉMON

TYPE: GRASS-POISON

The hooked stem behind its head lets Weepinbell hang from a tree branch to sleep. Sometimes it falls to the ground during the night.

HOW TO SAY IT: WEE-pin-bell
IMPERIAL HEIGHT: 3' 03"
METRIC HEIGHT: 1.0m

IMPERIAL WEIGHT: 14.1 lbs.
METRIC WEIGHT: 6.4 kg

POSSIBLE MOVES: Vine Whip, Growth, Wrap, Sleep Powder, Poison Powder, Stun Spore, Acid, Knock Off, Sweet Scent, Gastro Acid, Razor Leaf, Slam, Wring Out

EVOLUTION

Bellsprout › Weepinbell › Victreebel

Victreebel

#071

FLYCATCHER POKÉMON

TYPE: GRASS-POISON

Victreebel uses its long vine like a fishing lure, swishing and flicking it to draw prey closer to its gaping mouth.

HOW TO SAY IT: VICK-tree-bell
IMPERIAL HEIGHT: 5' 07"
METRIC HEIGHT: 1.7m

IMPERIAL WEIGHT: 34.2 lbs.
METRIC WEIGHT: 15.5 kg

POSSIBLE MOVES: Stockpile, Swallow, Spit Up, Vine Whip, Sleep Powder, Sweet Scent, Razor Leaf, Leaf Tornado, Leaf Storm, Leaf Blade

EVOLUTION

Bellsprout › Weepinbell › Victreebel

#072
Tentacool
JELLYFISH POKÉMON

TYPE: *WATER-POISON*

If a Tentacool spends too much time out of water, its body will dry out. In the sea, it can focus and redirect sunlight into energy beams.

HOW TO SAY IT: TEN-ta-cool
IMPERIAL HEIGHT: 2' 11"
METRIC HEIGHT: 0.9m

IMPERIAL WEIGHT: 100.3 lbs.
METRIC WEIGHT: 45.5 kg

POSSIBLE MOVES: Poison Sting, Supersonic, Constrict, Acid, Toxic Spikes, Bubble Beam, Wrap, Acid Spray, Barrier, Water Pulse, Poison Jab, Screech, Hex, Hydro Pump, Sludge Wave, Wring Out

EVOLUTION

Tentacool › Tentacruel

Tentacruel

JELLYFISH POKÉMON

TYPE: WATER-POISON

When the red orbs on Tentacruel's head glow, it's about to unleash a sonic blast that stirs up the sea. Its poisonous tentacles can extend to catch food.

HOW TO SAY IT: TEN-ta-crool

IMPERIAL HEIGHT: 5' 03"

METRIC HEIGHT: 1.6m

IMPERIAL WEIGHT: 121.3 lbs.

METRIC WEIGHT: 55.0 kg

POSSIBLE MOVES: Reflect Type, Poison Sting, Supersonic, Constrict, Acid, Toxic Spikes, Bubble Beam, Wrap, Acid Spray, Barrier, Water Pulse, Poison Jab, Screech, Hex, Hydro Pump, Sludge Wave, Wring Out

EVOLUTION

Tentacool › Tentacruel

(63)

Geodude

ROCK POKÉMON

TYPE: *ROCK-GROUND*

As a Geodude grows older, its rough edges are smoothed away. When it sleeps, it digs into the ground, where it resembles a rock.

HOW TO SAY IT: JEE-oh-dude

IMPERIAL HEIGHT: 1' 04"

METRIC HEIGHT: 0.4m

IMPERIAL WEIGHT: 44.1 lbs.

METRIC WEIGHT: 20.0 kg

POSSIBLE MOVES: Tackle, Defense Curl, Mud Sport, Rock Polish, Rollout, Magnitude, Rock Throw, Rock Blast, Smack Down, Self-Destruct, Bulldoze, Stealth Rock, Earthquake, Explosion, Double-Edge, Stone Edge

EVOLUTION

Geodude › Graveler › Golem

#075
Graveler
ROCK POKÉMON

TYPE: *ROCK-GROUND*

Graveler loves to eat rocks, and moss-covered rocks are a favorite snack. It will munch its way up the side of a mountain if it's hungry.

HOW TO SAY IT: GRAV-el-ler
IMPERIAL HEIGHT: 3' 03"
METRIC HEIGHT: 1.0m

IMPERIAL WEIGHT: 231.5 lbs.
METRIC WEIGHT: 105.0 kg

POSSIBLE MOVES: Tackle, Defense Curl, Mud Sport, Rock Polish, Rollout, Magnitude, Rock Throw, Rock Blast, Smack Down, Self-Destruct, Bulldoze, Stealth Rock, Earthquake, Explosion, Double-Edge, Stone Edge

EVOLUTION

Geodude › Graveler › Golem

#076
Golem
ROCK POKÉMON

TYPE: *ROCK-GROUND*

People who live on mountainsides sometimes dig grooves to keep Golem from rolling right into their houses.

HOW TO SAY IT: GO-lum
IMPERIAL HEIGHT: 4' 07"
METRIC HEIGHT: 1.4m

IMPERIAL WEIGHT: 661.4 lbs.
METRIC WEIGHT: 300.0 kg

POSSIBLE MOVES: Heavy Slam, Tackle, Defense Curl, Mud Sport, Rock Polish, Steamroller, Magnitude, Rock Throw, Rock Blast, Smack Down, Self-Destruct, Bulldoze, Stealth Rock, Earthquake, Explosion, Double-Edge, Stone Edge

EVOLUTION

Geodude › Graveler › Golem

(65)

#077
Ponyta
FIRE HORSE POKÉMON

TYPE: *FIRE*

At the beginning of its life, Ponyta's legs are too weak to hold it up. It quickly learns to run by chasing after its elders.

HOW TO SAY IT: POH-nee-tah
IMPERIAL HEIGHT: 3' 03"
METRIC HEIGHT: 1.0m

IMPERIAL WEIGHT: 66.1 lbs.
METRIC WEIGHT: 30.0 kg

POSSIBLE MOVES: Growl, Tackle, Tail Whip, Ember, Flame Wheel, Stomp, Flame Charge, Fire Spin, Take Down, Inferno, Agility, Fire Blast, Bounce, Flare Blitz

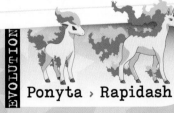

EVOLUTION

Ponyta › Rapidash

Rapidash

FIRE HORSE POKÉMON

TYPE: *FIRE*

Most of the time, Rapidash travels at a casual canter across the flat lands where it lives. When it breaks into a gallop, its mane blazes brightly.

HOW TO SAY IT: RAP-id-dash

IMPERIAL HEIGHT: 5' 07"

METRIC HEIGHT: 1.7m

IMPERIAL WEIGHT: 209.4 lbs.

METRIC WEIGHT: 95.0 kg

POSSIBLE MOVES: Poison Jab, Megahorn, Growl, Quick Attack, Tail Whip, Ember, Flame Wheel, Stomp, Flame Charge, Fire Spin, Take Down, Inferno, Agility, Fury Attack, Fire Blast, Bounce, Flare Blitz

EVOLUTION

Ponyta › Rapidash

(67)

#079
Slowpoke
DOPEY POKÉMON

TYPE: **WATER-PSYCHIC**

Slowpoke spends much of its time along the riverbank, where it uses its tail for fishing. Often, its mind wanders and it spends the whole day lazing about.

HOW TO SAY IT: SLOW-poke
IMPERIAL HEIGHT: 3' 11"
METRIC HEIGHT: 1.2m

IMPERIAL WEIGHT: 79.4 lbs.
METRIC WEIGHT: 36.0 kg

POSSIBLE MOVES: Curse, Yawn, Tackle, Growl, Water Gun, Confusion, Disable, Headbutt, Water Pulse, Zen Headbutt, Slack Off, Amnesia, Psychic, Rain Dance, Psych Up, Heal Pulse

EVOLUTION

Slowpoke › Slowbro

slowbro

HERMIT CRAB POKÉMON

TYPE: WATER-PSYCHIC

Because of the Shellder chomping on its tail, Slowbro can no longer spend its days fishing. It can swim to catch food, but it's not happy about that.

HOW TO SAY IT: SLOW-bro
IMPERIAL HEIGHT: 5' 03"
METRIC HEIGHT: 1.6m

IMPERIAL WEIGHT: 173.1 lbs.
METRIC WEIGHT: 78.5 kg

POSSIBLE MOVES: Heal Pulse, Curse, Yawn, Tackle, Growl, Water Gun, Confusion, Disable, Headbutt, Water Pulse, Zen Headbutt, Slack Off, Withdraw, Amnesia, Psychic, Rain Dance, Psych Up

EVOLUTION

Slowpoke › Slowbro

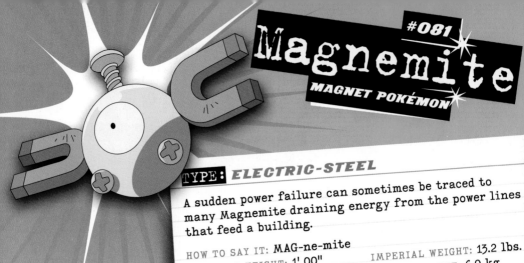

Magnemite

MAGNET POKÉMON

TYPE: ELECTRIC-STEEL

A sudden power failure can sometimes be traced to many Magnemite draining energy from the power lines that feed a building.

HOW TO SAY IT: MAG-ne-mite
IMPERIAL HEIGHT: 1' 00"
METRIC HEIGHT: 0.3m
IMPERIAL WEIGHT: 13.2 lbs.
METRIC WEIGHT: 6.0 kg

POSSIBLE MOVES: Tackle, Supersonic, Thunder Shock, Sonic Boom, Thunder Wave, Magnet Bomb, Spark, Mirror Shot, Metal Sound, Electro Ball, Flash Cannon, Screech, Discharge, Lock-On, Magnet Rise, Gyro Ball, Zap Cannon

EVOLUTION

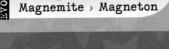

Magnemite › Magneton

Magneton

MAGNET POKÉMON

TYPE: ELECTRIC-STEEL

The magnetic field that surrounds Magneton can wreak havoc on electronics and other machines. Having this Pokémon around can be very bad for business.

HOW TO SAY IT: MAG-ne-ton
IMPERIAL HEIGHT: 3' 03"
METRIC HEIGHT: 1.0m
IMPERIAL WEIGHT: 132.3 lbs.
METRIC WEIGHT: 60.0 kg

POSSIBLE MOVES: Zap Cannon, Tri Attack, Tackle, Supersonic, Thunder Shock, Sonic Boom, Electric Terrain, Thunder Wave, Magnet Bomb, Spark, Mirror Shot, Metal Sound, Electro Ball, Flash Cannon, Screech, Discharge, Lock-On, Magnet Rise, Gyro Ball

EVOLUTION

Magnemite › Magneton

Farfetch'd

WILD DUCK POKÉMON

TYPE: NORMAL-FLYING

Farfetch'd always carries its trusty plant stalk. Sometimes, two of them will fight over a superior stalk.

HOW TO SAY IT: FAR-fetched
IMPERIAL HEIGHT: 2' 07"
METRIC HEIGHT: 0.8m

IMPERIAL WEIGHT: 33.1 lbs.
METRIC WEIGHT: 15.0 kg

POSSIBLE MOVES: Brave Bird, Poison Jab, Peck, Sand Attack, Leer, Fury Cutter, Fury Attack, Aerial Ace, Knock Off, Slash, Air Cutter, Swords Dance, Agility, Night Slash, Acrobatics, Feint, False Swipe, Air Slash

EVOLUTION

Does not evolve

#084

Doduo
TWIN BIRD POKÉMON

TYPE: NORMAL-FLYING

While one of Doduo's heads sleeps, the other stays alert to watch for danger. Its brains are identical.

HOW TO SAY IT: doe-DOO-oh
IMPERIAL HEIGHT: 4' 07"
METRIC HEIGHT: 1.4m

IMPERIAL WEIGHT: 86.4 lbs.
METRIC WEIGHT: 39.2 kg

POSSIBLE MOVES: Peck, Growl, Quick Attack, Rage, Fury Attack, Pursuit, Uproar, Acupressure, Double Hit, Agility, Drill Peck, Endeavor, Thrash

EVOLUTION

Doduo › Dodrio

Dodrio

TRIPLE BIRD POKÉMON

TYPE: NORMAL-FLYING

Dodrio has three heads, three hearts, and three sets of lungs. It can keep watch in all directions and run a long way without getting tired.

HOW TO SAY IT: doe-DREE-oh
IMPERIAL HEIGHT: 5' 11"
METRIC HEIGHT: 1.8m

IMPERIAL WEIGHT: 187.8 lbs.
METRIC WEIGHT: 85.2 kg

POSSIBLE MOVES: Pluck, Peck, Growl, Quick Attack, Rage, Fury Attack, Pursuit, Uproar, Acupressure, Tri Attack, Agility, Drill Peck, Endeavor, Thrash

EVOLUTION

Doduo › Dodrio

(73)

#086
Seel
SEA LION POKÉMON

TYPE: *WATER*

In frozen seas, Seel swims under the ice in search of food. It uses the point on its head to break through the ice when it comes up for air.

HOW TO SAY IT: SEEL
IMPERIAL HEIGHT: 3' 07"
METRIC HEIGHT: 1.1m
IMPERIAL WEIGHT: 198.4 lbs.
METRIC WEIGHT: 90.0 kg

POSSIBLE MOVES: Headbutt, Growl, Water Sport, Icy Wind, Encore, Ice Shard, Rest, Aqua Ring, Aurora Beam, Aqua Jet, Brine, Take Down, Dive, Aqua Tail, Ice Beam, Safeguard, Hail

EVOLUTION

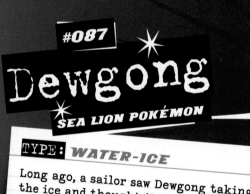

Seel › Dewgong

#087
Dewgong
SEA LION POKÉMON

TYPE: *WATER-ICE*

Long ago, a sailor saw Dewgong taking a nap on the ice and thought it was a mermaid. It sleeps best in the bitter cold.

HOW TO SAY IT: DOO-gong
IMPERIAL HEIGHT: 5' 07"
METRIC HEIGHT: 1.7m
IMPERIAL WEIGHT: 264.6 lbs.
METRIC WEIGHT: 120.0 kg

POSSIBLE MOVES: Headbutt, Growl, Signal Beam, Icy Wind, Encore, Ice Shard, Rest, Aqua Ring, Aurora Beam, Aqua Jet, Brine, Sheer Cold, Take Down, Dive, Aqua Tail, Ice Beam, Safeguard, Hail

EVOLUTION

Seel › Dewgong

#088
Grimer
SLUDGE POKÉMON

TYPE: POISON

Because its body is like sludge, Grimer can squeeze itself into small openings like sewer pipes. The fluid it gives off is full of germs.

HOW TO SAY IT: GRY-mur
IMPERIAL HEIGHT: 2' 11"
METRIC HEIGHT: 0.9m
IMPERIAL WEIGHT: 66.1 lbs.
METRIC WEIGHT: 30.0 kg

POSSIBLE MOVES: Poison Gas, Pound, Harden, Mud-Slap, Disable, Minimize, Sludge, Mud Bomb, Fling, Screech, Sludge Bomb, Acid Armor, Sludge Wave, Gunk Shot, Memento

EVOLUTION
Grimer › Muk

#089
Muk
SLUDGE POKÉMON

TYPE: POISON

Muk really stinks. The fluid it oozes gives off a terrible smell and pollutes clean water. Cities with a trash problem may also find they have a Muk problem.

HOW TO SAY IT: MUCK
IMPERIAL HEIGHT: 3' 11"
METRIC HEIGHT: 1.2m
IMPERIAL WEIGHT: 66.1 lbs.
METRIC WEIGHT: 30.0 kg

POSSIBLE MOVES: Poison Gas, Pound, Harden, Mud-Slap, Disable, Minimize, Sludge, Mud Bomb, Fling, Screech, Sludge Bomb, Acid Armor, Sludge Wave, Gunk Shot, Memento

EVOLUTION
Grimer › Muk

Shellder
#090
BIVALVE POKÉMON

TYPE: *WATER*

When Shellder's shell is closed, its large tongue tends to hang out. It uses its tongue as a shovel to dig a nest in the sand.

HOW TO SAY IT: SHELL-der
IMPERIAL HEIGHT: 1' 00"
METRIC HEIGHT: 0.3m

IMPERIAL WEIGHT: 8.8 lbs.
METRIC WEIGHT: 4.0 kg

POSSIBLE MOVES: Tackle, Withdraw, Supersonic, Icicle Spear, Protect, Leer, Clamp, Ice Shard, Razor Shell, Aurora Beam, Whirlpool, Brine, Iron Defense, Ice Beam, Shell Smash, Hydro Pump

EVOLUTION

Shellder › Cloyster

#091
Cloyster
BIVALVE POKÉMON

TYPE: *WATER-ICE*

By sucking in water and then shooting it out, Cloyster can propel itself through the sea. It also uses this method to fire its shell spikes in battle.

HOW TO SAY IT: CLOY-ster
IMPERIAL HEIGHT: 4' 11"
METRIC HEIGHT: 1.5m

IMPERIAL WEIGHT: 292.1 lbs.
METRIC WEIGHT: 132.5 kg

POSSIBLE MOVES: Hydro Pump, Shell Smash, Toxic Spikes, Withdraw, Supersonic, Protect, Aurora Beam, Spike Cannon, Spikes, Icicle Crash

EVOLUTION

Shellder › Cloyster

Gastly

GAS POKÉMON

TYPE: *GHOST-POISON*

Gastly's body is made of gas clouds that can be disrupted by strong winds. Groups of them sometimes huddle close to a house for protection.

HOW TO SAY IT: GAST-lee
IMPERIAL HEIGHT: 4' 03"
METRIC HEIGHT: 1.3m

IMPERIAL WEIGHT: 0.2 lbs.
METRIC WEIGHT: 0.1 kg

POSSIBLE MOVES: Hypnosis, Lick, Spite, Mean Look, Curse, Night Shade, Confuse Ray, Sucker Punch, Payback, Shadow Ball, Dream Eater, Dark Pulse, Destiny Bond, Hex, Nightmare

EVOLUTION

Gastly › Haunter › Gengar

#093

Haunter

GAS POKÉMON

TYPE: *GHOST-POISON*

Don't ever let a Haunter lick you! Its ghostly tongue can steal your life energy.

HOW TO SAY IT: HAUNT-ur
IMPERIAL HEIGHT: 5' 03"
METRIC HEIGHT: 1.6m

IMPERIAL WEIGHT: 0.2 lbs.
METRIC WEIGHT: 0.1 kg

POSSIBLE MOVES: Hypnosis, Lick, Spite, Mean Look, Curse, Night Shade, Confuse Ray, Sucker Punch, Payback, Shadow Ball, Dream Eater, Dark Pulse, Destiny Bond, Hex, Nightmare

EVOLUTION

Gastly › Haunter › Gengar

#094

Gengar

SHADOW POKÉMON

TYPE: GHOST-POISON

If your shadow suddenly runs away, it might be a Gengar stalking you through the darkness.

HOW TO SAY IT: GHEN-gar
IMPERIAL HEIGHT: 4' 11"
METRIC HEIGHT: 1.5m

IMPERIAL WEIGHT: 89.3 lbs.
METRIC WEIGHT: 40.5 kg

POSSIBLE MOVES: Hypnosis, Lick, Spite, Mean Look, Curse, Night Shade, Confuse Ray, Sucker Punch, Payback, Shadow Ball, Dream Eater, Dark Pulse, Destiny Bond, Hex, Nightmare

EVOLUTION

Gastly › Haunter › Gengar

Onix

ROCK SNAKE POKÉMON

TYPE: ROCK-GROUND

Thanks to its internal magnet, Onix never loses its way while boring through the ground. Its body grows smoother with age as the rough edges wear away.

HOW TO SAY IT: ON-icks

IMPERIAL HEIGHT: 28' 10"

METRIC HEIGHT: 8.8m

IMPERIAL WEIGHT: 463.0 lbs.

METRIC WEIGHT: 210.0 kg

POSSIBLE MOVES: Mud Sport, Tackle, Harden, Bind, Curse, Rock Throw, Rock Tomb, Rage, Stealth Rock, Rock Polish, Gyro Ball, Smack Down, Dragon Breath, Slam, Screech, Rock Slide, Sand Tomb, Iron Tail, Dig, Stone Edge, Double-Edge, Sandstorm

Does not evolve

Drowzee
#096
HYPNOSIS POKÉMON

TYPE: *PSYCHIC*

Ever wake up with an itchy nose? It might be because a Drowzee was lurking nearby, trying to draw out your dreams.

HOW TO SAY IT: DROW-zee
IMPERIAL HEIGHT: 3' 03"
METRIC HEIGHT: 1.0m

IMPERIAL WEIGHT: 71.4 lbs
METRIC WEIGHT: 32.4 kg

POSSIBLE MOVES: Pound, Hypnosis, Disable, Confusion, Headbutt, Poison Gas, Meditate, Psybeam, Psych Up, Synchronoise, Zen Headbutt, Swagger, Psychic, Nasty Plot, Psyshock, Future Sight

EVOLUTION

Drowzee › Hypno

#097
Hypno
HYPNOSIS POKÉMON

TYPE: *PSYCHIC*

As Hypno's pendulum swings and shines, anyone watching falls into a hypnotic trance. To enhance the effect, it always keeps the pendulum polished.

HOW TO SAY IT: HIP-no
IMPERIAL HEIGHT: 5' 03"
METRIC HEIGHT: 1.6m

IMPERIAL WEIGHT: 166.7 lbs.
METRIC WEIGHT: 75.6 kg

POSSIBLE MOVES: Nightmare, Switcheroo, Pound, Hypnosis, Disable, Confusion, Headbutt, Poison Gas, Meditate, Psybeam, Psych Up, Synchronoise, Zen Headbutt, Swagger, Psychic, Nasty Plot, Psyshock, Future Sight

EVOLUTION

Drowzee › Hypno

#098
Krabby
RIVER CRAB POKÉMON

TYPE: WATER

Krabby dig holes in sandy beaches to make their homes. When the food supply is limited, they sometimes fight over territory.

HOW TO SAY IT: **KRAB-ee**
IMPERIAL HEIGHT: 1' 04"
METRIC HEIGHT: 0.4m
IMPERIAL WEIGHT: 14.3 lbs.
METRIC WEIGHT: 6.5 kg

POSSIBLE MOVES: Mud Sport, Bubble, Vice Grip, Leer, Harden, Bubble Beam, Mud Shot, Metal Claw, Stomp, Protect, Guillotine, Slam, Brine, Crabhammer, Flail

EVOLUTION

Krabby › Kingler

#099
Kingler
PINCER POKÉMON

TYPE: WATER

When one Kingler waves to another with its giant claw, it's sending a message. They can't hold long conversations this way, though, because waving those heavy claws is tiring.

HOW TO SAY IT: **KING-lur**
IMPERIAL HEIGHT: 4' 03"
METRIC HEIGHT: 1.3m
IMPERIAL WEIGHT: 132.3 lbs.
METRIC WEIGHT: 60.0 kg

POSSIBLE MOVES: Wide Guard, Mud Sport, Bubble, Vice Grip, Leer, Harden, Bubble Beam, Mud Shot, Metal Claw, Stomp, Protect, Guillotine, Slam, Brine, Crabhammer, Flail

EVOLUTION

Krabby › Kingler

Voltorb

#100

BALL POKÉMON

TYPE: *ELECTRIC*

Voltorb looks a lot like a Poké Ball, and it was first spotted at a Poké Ball factory. What's the connection? Nobody knows.

HOW TO SAY IT: VOLT-orb
IMPERIAL HEIGHT: 1' 08"
METRIC HEIGHT: 0.5m
IMPERIAL WEIGHT: 22.9 lbs.
METRIC WEIGHT: 10.4 kg

POSSIBLE MOVES: Charge, Tackle, Sonic Boom, Eerie Impulse, Spark, Rollout, Screech, Charge Beam, Light Screen, Electro Ball, Self-Destruct, Swift, Magnet Rise, Gyro Ball, Explosion, Mirror Coat

EVOLUTION

Voltorb › Electrode

#101

Electrode

BALL POKÉMON

TYPE: *ELECTRIC*

Electrode feeds by absorbing electricity, often from power plants or lightning storms. If it eats too much at once, it explodes.

HOW TO SAY IT: ee-LECK-trode
IMPERIAL HEIGHT: 3' 11"
METRIC HEIGHT: 1.2m
IMPERIAL WEIGHT: 146.8 lbs.
METRIC WEIGHT: 66.6 kg

POSSIBLE MOVES: Magnetic Flux, Charge, Tackle, Sonic Boom, Eerie Impulse, Spark, Rollout, Screech, Charge Beam, Light Screen, Electro Ball, Self-Destruct, Swift, Magnet Rise, Gyro Ball, Explosion, Mirror Coat

EVOLUTION

Voltorb › Electrode

Exeggcute

EGG POKÉMON

TYPE: GRASS-PSYCHIC

The six eggs that make up Exeggcute's body spin around a common center. When the eggs begin to crack, this Pokémon is ready to evolve.

HOW TO SAY IT: ECKS-egg-cute
IMPERIAL HEIGHT: 1' 04"
METRIC HEIGHT: 0.4m

IMPERIAL WEIGHT: 5.5 lbs.
METRIC WEIGHT: 2.5 kg

POSSIBLE MOVES: Barrage, Uproar, Hypnosis, Reflect, Leech Seed, Bullet Seed, Stun Spore, Poison Powder, Sleep Powder, Confusion, Worry Seed, Natural Gift, Solar Beam, Extrasensory, Bestow

EVOLUTION

Exeggcute › Exeggutor

#103
Exeggutor
COCONUT POKÉMON

TYPE: *GRASS-PSYCHIC*

A tropical Pokémon, Exeggutor has three heads that keep growing when they get enough sun. Exeggcute are thought to form from the fallen heads of Exeggutor.

HOW TO SAY IT: ecks-EGG-u-tore
IMPERIAL HEIGHT: 6' 07"
METRIC HEIGHT: 2.0m

IMPERIAL WEIGHT: 264.6 lbs.
METRIC WEIGHT: 120.0 kg

POSSIBLE MOVES: Seed Bomb, Barrage, Hypnosis, Confusion, Stomp, Psyshock, Egg Bomb, Wood Hammer, Leaf Storm

EVOLUTION

Exeggcute › Exeggutor

Cubone

LONELY POKÉMON

TYPE: GROUND

When Cubone looks at the full moon, it often sees an image of its lost mother. Its tears leave stains on the skull it wears.

HOW TO SAY IT: CUE-bone
IMPERIAL HEIGHT: 1' 04"
METRIC HEIGHT: 0.4m
IMPERIAL WEIGHT: 14.3 lbs.
METRIC WEIGHT: 6.5 kg

POSSIBLE MOVES: Growl, Tail Whip, Bone Club, Headbutt, Leer, Focus Energy, Bonemerang, Rage, False Swipe, Thrash, Fling, Bone Rush, Endeavor, Double-Edge, Retaliate

EVOLUTION
Cubone › Marowak

Marowak

#105

BONE KEEPER POKÉMON

TYPE: GROUND

After overcoming its grief and evolving, Marowak has become extremely tough. Its spirit, tempered by adversity, can withstand just about anything.

HOW TO SAY IT: MAR-oh-wack
IMPERIAL HEIGHT: 3' 03"
METRIC HEIGHT: 1.0m
IMPERIAL WEIGHT: 99.2 lbs.
METRIC WEIGHT: 45.0 kg

POSSIBLE MOVES: Growl, Tail Whip, Bone Club, Headbutt, Leer, Focus Energy, Bonemerang, Rage, False Swipe, Thrash, Fling, Bone Rush, Endeavor, Double-Edge, Retaliate

EVOLUTION
Cubone › Marowak

Hitmonlee

#106

KICKING POKÉMON

TYPE: *FIGHTING*

Hitmonlee can extend its legs like springs to deliver kicks with tremendous force. It's always careful to stretch and loosen up after battle.

HOW TO SAY IT: HIT-mon-LEE
IMPERIAL HEIGHT: 4' 11"
METRIC HEIGHT: 1.5m

IMPERIAL WEIGHT: 109.8 lbs.
METRIC WEIGHT: 49.8 kg

POSSIBLE MOVES: Revenge, Double Kick, Meditate, Rolling Kick, Jump Kick, Brick Break, Focus Energy, Feint, High Jump Kick, Mind Reader, Foresight, Wide Guard, Blaze Kick, Endure, Mega Kick, Close Combat, Reversal

EVOLUTION

Hitmonlee › Hitmonchan

#107

Hitmonchan

PUNCHING POKÉMON

TYPE: *FIGHTING*

Hitmonchan has the fighting spirit of a world-class boxer. It's extremely driven and never gives up.

HOW TO SAY IT: HIT-mon-CHAN
IMPERIAL HEIGHT: 4' 07"
METRIC HEIGHT: 1.4m

IMPERIAL WEIGHT: 110.7 lbs.
METRIC WEIGHT: 50.2 kg

POSSIBLE MOVES: Revenge, Comet Punch, Agility, Pursuit, Mach Punch, Bullet Punch, Feint, Vacuum Wave, Quick Guard, Thunder Punch, Ice Punch, Fire Punch, Sky Uppercut, Mega Punch, Detect, Focus Punch, Counter, Close Combat

EVOLUTION

Hitmonlee › Hitmonchan

#108
Lickitung

LICKING POKÉMON

TYPE: *NORMAL*

Lickitung learns about new things by licking them to discover their taste and texture. Sour tastes are not its favorite.

HOW TO SAY IT: LICK-it-tung
IMPERIAL HEIGHT: 3' 11"
METRIC HEIGHT: 1.2m

IMPERIAL WEIGHT: 144.4 lbs.
METRIC WEIGHT: 65.5 kg

POSSIBLE MOVES: Lick, Supersonic, Defense Curl, Knock Off, Wrap, Stomp, Disable, Slam, Rollout, Chip Away, Me First, Refresh, Screech, Power Whip, Wring Out

EVOLUTION

Does not evolve

(87)

Koffing #109

POISON GAS POKÉMON

TYPE: *POISON*

The gases that fill Koffing's body are extremely toxic. When it's under attack, it releases this poisonous gas from jets on its surface.

HOW TO SAY IT: **KOFF-ing**
IMPERIAL HEIGHT: 2' 00"
METRIC HEIGHT: 0.6m

IMPERIAL WEIGHT: 2.2 lbs.
METRIC WEIGHT: 1.0 kg

POSSIBLE MOVES: Poison Gas, Tackle, Smog, Smokescreen, Assurance, Clear Smog, Self-Destruct, Sludge, Haze, Gyro Ball, Explosion, Sludge Bomb, Destiny Bond, Memento

EVOLUTION

Koffing › Weezing

#110

Weezing

POISON GAS POKÉMON

TYPE: *POISON*

Rotting food gives off a noxious gas that attracts Weezing. Its twin bodies take turns inflating and deflating to keep its poisonous gases churning.

HOW TO SAY IT: **WEEZ-ing**
IMPERIAL HEIGHT: 3' 11"
METRIC HEIGHT: 1.2m

IMPERIAL WEIGHT: 20.9 lbs.
METRIC WEIGHT: 9.5 kg

POSSIBLE MOVES: Poison Gas, Tackle, Smog, Smokescreen, Assurance, Clear Smog, Self-Destruct, Sludge, Haze, Double Hit, Explosion, Sludge Bomb, Destiny Bond, Memento

(88)

EVOLUTION

Koffing › Weezing

#111
Rhyhorn
SPIKES POKÉMON

TYPE: *GROUND-ROCK*

A charging Rhyhorn is so single-minded that it doesn't think about anything else until it demolishes its target.

HOW TO SAY IT: RHY-horn
IMPERIAL HEIGHT: 3' 03"
METRIC HEIGHT: 1.0m
IMPERIAL WEIGHT: 253.5 lbs.
METRIC WEIGHT: 115.0 kg

POSSIBLE MOVES: Horn Attack, Tail Whip, Stomp, Fury Attack, Scary Face, Rock Blast, Bulldoze, Chip Away, Take Down, Drill Run, Stone Edge, Earthquake, Horn Drill, Megahorn

EVOLUTION

Rhyhorn › Rhydon

#112
Rhydon
DRILL POKÉMON

TYPE: *GROUND-ROCK*

Rhydon's horn, which it uses as a drill, is hard enough to crush diamonds. Its hide is like armor, and it can run right through molten lava without feeling a thing.

HOW TO SAY IT: RYE-don
IMPERIAL HEIGHT: 6' 03"
METRIC HEIGHT: 1.9m
IMPERIAL WEIGHT: 264.6 lbs.
METRIC WEIGHT: 120.0 kg

POSSIBLE MOVES: Megahorn, Horn Drill, Horn Attack, Tail Whip, Stomp, Fury Attack, Scary Face, Rock Blast, Bulldoze, Chip Away, Take Down, Hammer Arm, Drill Run, Stone Edge, Earthquake

EVOLUTION
Rhyhorn › Rhydon

Chansey

EGG POKÉMON

TYPE: *NORMAL*

The eggs Chansey produces every day are full of nutrition and flavor. Even people suffering a loss of appetite eat them up with delight.

HOW TO SAY IT: **CHAN-see**
IMPERIAL HEIGHT: **3' 07"**
METRIC HEIGHT: **1.1m**

IMPERIAL WEIGHT: **76.3 lbs.**
METRIC WEIGHT: **34.6 kg**

POSSIBLE MOVES: **Defense Curl, Pound, Growl, Tail Whip, Refresh, Double Slap, Softboiled, Bestow, Minimize, Take Down, Sing, Fling, Heal Pulse, Egg Bomb, Light Screen, Healing Wish, Double-Edge**

EVOLUTION

Does not evolve

Tangela
VINE POKÉMON

TYPE: GRASS

If grabbed by an attacker, Tangela can break away and leave the foe with a handful of vines. The vines grow back within a day.

HOW TO SAY IT: **TANG-ghel-a**
IMPERIAL HEIGHT: **3' 03"**
METRIC HEIGHT: **1.0m**

IMPERIAL WEIGHT: **77.2 lbs.**
METRIC WEIGHT: **35.0 kg**

POSSIBLE MOVES: **Ingrain, Constrict, Sleep Powder, Absorb, Growth, Poison Powder, Vine Whip, Bind, Mega Drain, Stun Spore, Knock Off, Ancient Power, Natural Gift, Slam, Tickle, Wring Out, Power Whip**

Does not evolve

Kangaskhan

PARENT POKÉMON

TYPE: NORMAL

A little Kangaskhan playing on its own should be left alone. The Parent Pokémon always keeps careful watch and will attack any aggressor.

HOW TO SAY IT: KANG-gas-con

IMPERIAL HEIGHT: 7' 0"

METRIC HEIGHT: 2.2m

IMPERIAL WEIGHT: 176.4 lbs.

METRIC WEIGHT: 80.0 kg

POSSIBLE MOVES: Comet Punch, Leer, Fake Out, Tail Whip, Bite, Double Hit, Rage, Mega Punch, Chip Away, Dizzy Punch, Crunch, Endure, Outrage, Sucker Punch, Reversal

EVOLUTION

Does not evolve

Horsea

DRAGON POKÉMON

TYPE: *WATER*

Horsea wraps its tail around solid objects on the seafloor to avoid being swept away in a strong current. When threatened, it spits a cloud of ink to cover its escape.

HOW TO SAY IT: HOR-see
IMPERIAL HEIGHT: 1' 04"
METRIC HEIGHT: 0.4m

IMPERIAL WEIGHT: 17.6 lbs.
METRIC WEIGHT: 8.0 kg

POSSIBLE MOVES: Water Gun, Smokescreen, Leer, Bubble, Focus Energy, Bubble Beam, Agility, Twister, Brine, Hydro Pump, Dragon Dance, Dragon Pulse

EVOLUTION

Horsea › Seadra

Seadra

DRAGON POKÉMON

TYPE: *WATER*

When Seadra spins around in the water, it can cause a whirlpool with enough force to capsize a small boat. It sleeps among coral branches.

HOW TO SAY IT: SEE-dra
IMPERIAL HEIGHT: 3' 11"
METRIC HEIGHT: 1.2m

IMPERIAL WEIGHT: 55.1 lbs.
METRIC WEIGHT: 25.0 kg

POSSIBLE MOVES: Water Gun, Smokescreen, Leer, Bubble, Focus Energy, Bubble Beam, Agility, Twister, Brine, Hydro Pump, Dragon Dance, Dragon Pulse

EVOLUTION

Horsea › Seadra

Goldeen
#118
GOLDFISH POKÉMON

TYPE: *WATER*

Goldeen's long, elegant fins wave gracefully in the water. It's hard to keep this lovely Pokémon in an aquarium, because its horn can break through thick glass.

HOW TO SAY IT: GOL-deen
IMPERIAL HEIGHT: 2' 00"
METRIC HEIGHT: 0.6m

IMPERIAL WEIGHT: 33.1 lbs.
METRIC WEIGHT: 15.0 kg

POSSIBLE MOVES: Peck, Tail Whip, Water Sport, Supersonic, Horn Attack, Water Pulse, Flail, Aqua Ring, Fury Attack, Waterfall, Horn Drill, Agility, Soak, Megahorn

EVOLUTION

Goldeen › Seaking

#119
Seaking
GOLDFISH POKÉMON

TYPE: *WATER*

Male Seaking become brilliantly colored during the autumn, when they perform their courtship dance. Matched pairs take turns keeping watch over their nests.

HOW TO SAY IT: SEE-king
IMPERIAL HEIGHT: 4' 03"
METRIC HEIGHT: 1.3m

IMPERIAL WEIGHT: 86.0 lbs.
METRIC WEIGHT: 39.0 kg

POSSIBLE MOVES: Megahorn, Poison Jab, Peck, Tail Whip, Water Sport, Supersonic, Horn Attack, Water Pulse, Flail, Aqua Ring, Fury Attack, Waterfall, Horn Drill, Agility, Soak

EVOLUTION

Goldeen › Seaking

#120
Staryu
STAR SHAPE POKÉMON

TYPE: WATER

Staryu's red core glows brightly in the dark. When it flashes this light, it is said to be communing with the stars.

HOW TO SAY IT: STAHR-you
IMPERIAL HEIGHT: 2' 07"
METRIC HEIGHT: 0.8m

IMPERIAL WEIGHT: 76.1 lbs.
METRIC WEIGHT: 34.5 kg

POSSIBLE MOVES: Tackle, Harden, Water Gun, Rapid Spin, Recover, Camouflage, Swift, Bubble Beam, Minimize, Gyro Ball, Light Screen, Brine, Reflect Type, Power Gem, Cosmic Power, Hydro Pump

EVOLUTION

Staryu › Starmie

(95)

#121
Starmie
MYSTERIOUS POKÉMON

TYPE: *WATER-PSYCHIC*

Because of the glowing rainbow of colors produced by Starmie's core, this Pokémon is known as "the gem of the sea." It spins its body like a propeller to swim.

HOW TO SAY IT: STAR-mee
IMPERIAL HEIGHT: 3' 07"
METRIC HEIGHT: 1.1m

IMPERIAL WEIGHT: 176.4 lbs.
METRIC WEIGHT: 80.0 kg

POSSIBLE MOVES: Hydro Pump, Water Gun, Rapid Spin, Recover, Swift, Confuse Ray

EVOLUTION

Staryu › Starmie

#122
Mr. Mime

BARRIER POKÉMON

TYPE: *PSYCHIC*

Sometimes, Mr. Mime's gestures convince an onlooker that the invisible thing it's miming actually exists. Then, that thing becomes real.

HOW TO SAY IT: MIS-ter MIME
IMPERIAL HEIGHT: 4' 03"
METRIC HEIGHT: 1.3m

IMPERIAL WEIGHT: 120.1 lbs.
METRIC WEIGHT: 54.5 kg

POSSIBLE MOVES: Misty Terrain, Magical Leaf, Quick Guard, Wide Guard, Power Swap, Guard Swap, Barrier, Confusion, Copycat, Meditate, Double Slap, Mimic, Psywave, Encore, Light Screen, Reflect, Psybeam, Substitute, Recycle, Trick, Psychic, Role Play, Baton Pass, Safeguard

EVOLUTION

Does not evolve

(97)

#123

Scyther

MANTIS POKÉMON

TYPE: *BUG-FLYING*

With its impressive speed and razor-sharp scythes, Scyther is a formidable opponent. It can slash through a log with one blow.

HOW TO SAY IT: SY-thur
IMPERIAL HEIGHT: 4' 11"
METRIC HEIGHT: 1.5m

IMPERIAL WEIGHT: 123.5 lbs.
METRIC WEIGHT: 56.0 kg

POSSIBLE MOVES: Vacuum Wave, Quick Attack, Leer, Focus Energy, Pursuit, False Swipe, Agility, Wing Attack, Fury Cutter, Slash, Razor Wind, Double Team, X-Scissor, Night Slash, Double Hit, Air Slash, Swords Dance, Feint

EVOLUTION

Does not evolve

#124
Jynx

HUMAN SHAPE POKÉMON

TYPE: *ICE-PSYCHIC*

Jynx has a hypnotic, rhythmic walk that makes it look like it's dancing. People who watch it move often find themselves dancing along.

HOW TO SAY IT: JINX
IMPERIAL HEIGHT: 4' 07"
METRIC HEIGHT: 1.4m

IMPERIAL WEIGHT: 89.5 lbs.
METRIC WEIGHT: 40.6 kg

POSSIBLE MOVES: Draining Kiss, Perish Song, Pound, Lick, Lovely Kiss, Powder Snow, Double Slap, Ice Punch, Heart Stamp, Mean Look, Fake Tears, Wake-Up Slap, Avalanche, Body Slam, Wring Out, Perish Song, Blizzard

EVOLUTION

Does not evolve

Electabuzz

ELECTRIC POKÉMON

TYPE: ELECTRIC

During thunderstorms, Electabuzz climb to high places, hoping to be struck by lightning. Because they can absorb the bolts safely, they sometimes act as lightning rods.

HOW TO SAY IT: eh-LECK-ta-buzz

IMPERIAL HEIGHT: 3' 0"

METRIC HEIGHT: 1.1m

IMPERIAL WEIGHT: 66.1 lbs.

METRIC WEIGHT: 30.0 kg

POSSIBLE MOVES: Quick Attack, Leer, Thunder Shock, Low Kick, Swift, Shock Wave, Light Screen, Electro Ball, Thunder Punch, Discharge, Thunderbolt, Screech, Thunder

EVOLUTION

Does not evolve

Magmar

SPITFIRE POKÉMON

TYPE: FIRE

When Magmar releases bursts of flame during a battle, any nearby plant life is in danger of catching fire.

HOW TO SAY IT: MAG-marr

IMPERIAL HEIGHT: 4' 03"
METRIC HEIGHT: 1.3m

IMPERIAL WEIGHT: 98.1 lbs.
METRIC WEIGHT: 44.5 kg

POSSIBLE MOVES: Smog, Leer, Ember, Smokescreen, Feint Attack, Fire Spin, Confuse Ray, Flame Burst, Fire Punch, Lava Plume, Flamethrower, Sunny Day, Fire Blast

EVOLUTION

Does not evolve

(101)

Pinsir

STAG BEETLE POKÉMON

TYPE: *BUG*

When its strong pincer gets a grip, Pinsir can lift an enemy much bigger than itself. The thorns that line its horns dig into its opponent, making it hard to get away.

HOW TO SAY IT: PIN-sir
IMPERIAL HEIGHT: 4' 11"
METRIC HEIGHT: 1.5m

IMPERIAL WEIGHT: 121.3 lbs.
METRIC WEIGHT: 55.0 kg

POSSIBLE MOVES: Vice Grip, Focus Energy, Bind, Seismic Toss, Harden, Revenge, Brick Break, Vital Throw, Submission, X-Scissor, Storm Throw, Thrash, Swords Dance, Superpower, Guillotine

EVOLUTION

Does not evolve

#128
Tauros
WILD BULL POKÉMON

TYPE: NORMAL

Tauros just isn't happy unless it's battling. If nobody's up for the challenge, it blows off steam by charging at trees and knocking them over.

HOW TO SAY IT: TORE-ros
IMPERIAL HEIGHT: 4' 07"
METRIC HEIGHT: 1.4m

IMPERIAL WEIGHT: 194.9 lbs.
METRIC WEIGHT: 88.4 kg

POSSIBLE MOVES: Tackle, Tail Whip, Rage, Horn Attack, Scary Face, Pursuit, Rest, Payback, Work Up, Zen Headbutt, Take Down, Swagger, Thrash, Giga Impact

EVOLUTION

Does not evolve

(103)

#129
Magikarp
FISH POKÉMON

TYPE: WATER

Though Magikarp is an exceptionally weak Pokémon when it comes to battle skills, it has an extremely strong constitution. It can live in the most polluted of water.

HOW TO SAY IT: MADGE-eh-karp
IMPERIAL HEIGHT: 2' 11"
METRIC HEIGHT: 0.9m

IMPERIAL WEIGHT: 22.0 lbs.
METRIC WEIGHT: 10.0 kg

POSSIBLE MOVES: Splash, Tackle, Flail

EVOLUTION

Magikarp › Gyarados

#130

Gyarados

ATROCIOUS POKÉMON

TYPE: *WATER-FLYING*

After evolving, Gyarados experiences a shift in the cellular structure of its brain. This may explain why it is so violent, sometimes going on month-long rampages.

HOW TO SAY IT: GARE-uh-dos
IMPERIAL HEIGHT: 21' 04"
METRIC HEIGHT: 6.5m

IMPERIAL WEIGHT: 518.1 lbs.
METRIC WEIGHT: 235.0 kg

POSSIBLE MOVES: Thrash, Bite, Dragon Rage, Leer, Twister, Ice Fang, Aqua Tail, Rain Dance, Hydro Pump, Dragon Dance, Hyper Beam

EVOLUTION

Magikarp › Gyarados

(105)

Lapras

TRANSPORT POKÉMON

TYPE: *WATER-ICE*

When a Lapras sings a sad song at twilight, it's said to be looking for other Lapras. Because of human activity, these Pokémon are growing more rare.

HOW TO SAY IT: LAP-rus
IMPERIAL HEIGHT: 8' 02"
METRIC HEIGHT: 2.5m

IMPERIAL WEIGHT: 485.0 lbs.
METRIC WEIGHT: 220.0 kg

POSSIBLE MOVES: Sing, Growl, Water Gun, Mist, Confuse Ray, Ice Shard, Water Pulse, Body Slam, Rain Dance, Perish Song, Ice Beam, Brine, Safeguard, Hydro Pump, Sheer Cold

EVOLUTION

Does not evolve

#132
Ditto
TRANSFORM POKÉMON

TYPE: NORMAL

Ditto can alter the structure of its cells to change its shape. This works best if it has an example to copy—if it tries to copy another shape from memory, it sometimes gets things wrong.

HOW TO SAY IT: **DIT-toe**
IMPERIAL HEIGHT: **1' 00"**
METRIC HEIGHT: **0.3m**

IMPERIAL WEIGHT: **8.8 lbs.**
METRIC WEIGHT: **4.0 kg**

POSSIBLE MOVE: **Transform**

EVOLUTION

Does not evolve

#133
Eevee
EVOLUTION POKÉMON

TYPE: *NORMAL*

The amazingly adaptive Eevee can evolve into many different Pokémon depending on its environment. Certain stones can trigger its evolution.

HOW TO SAY IT: Eee-vee
IMPERIAL HEIGHT: 1' 00"
METRIC HEIGHT: 0.3m

IMPERIAL WEIGHT: 14.3 lbs.
METRIC WEIGHT: 6.5 kg

POSSIBLE MOVES: Helping Hand, Growl, Tackle, Tail Whip, Sand Attack, Baby-Doll Eyes, Swift, Quick Attack, Bite, Refresh, Covet, Take Down, Charm, Baton Pass, Double-Edge, Last Resort, Trump Card

EVOLUTION

Eevee

Jolteon Vaporeon Flareon

#134
Vaporeon
BUBBLE JET POKÉMON

TYPE: WATER

With its gills and fins, Vaporeon has adapted to an aquatic life. It can control its watery habitat with ease.

HOW TO SAY IT: vay-POUR-ree-on
IMPERIAL HEIGHT: 3' 03"
METRIC HEIGHT: 1.0m

IMPERIAL WEIGHT: 63.9 lbs.
METRIC WEIGHT: 29.0 kg

POSSIBLE MOVES: Helping Hand, Tackle, Tail Whip, Sand Attack, Water Gun, Quick Attack, Water Pulse, Aurora Beam, Aqua Ring, Acid Armor, Haze, Muddy Water, Last Resort, Hydro Pump

EVOLUTION

Eevee › Vaporeon

Jolteon

#135

LIGHTNING POKÉMON

TYPE: *ELECTRIC*

Jolteon's fur carries a static charge, and its body generates electricity. It can channel this electricity during battle to call down a thunderbolt!

HOW TO SAY IT: JOL-tee-on
IMPERIAL HEIGHT: 2' 07"
METRIC HEIGHT: 0.8m
IMPERIAL WEIGHT: 54.0 lbs.
METRIC WEIGHT: 24.5 kg

POSSIBLE MOVES: Helping Hand, Tackle, Tail Whip, Sand Attack, Thunder Shock, Quick Attack, Double Kick, Thunder Fang, Pin Missile, Agility, Thunder Wave, Discharge, Last Resort, Thunder

EVOLUTION

Eevee › Jolteon

#136

Flareon

FLAME POKÉMON

TYPE: *FIRE*

Flareon's body can become very hot, so it fluffs out its soft fur to release excess heat into its surroundings. Even so, it can reach more than 1,600 degrees Fahrenheit.

HOW TO SAY IT: FLAIR-ee-on
IMPERIAL HEIGHT: 2' 11"
METRIC HEIGHT: 0.9m
IMPERIAL WEIGHT: 55.1 lbs.
METRIC WEIGHT: 25.0 kg

POSSIBLE MOVES: Helping Hand, Tackle, Tail Whip, Sand Attack, Ember, Quick Attack, Bite, Fire Fang, Fire Spin, Scary Face, Smog, Lava Plume, Last Resort, Flare Blitz

EVOLUTION

Eevee › Flareon

#137
Porygon
VIRTUAL POKÉMON

TYPE: NORMAL

Porygon was created from programming code, and it can return to that form to navigate cyberspace. It can't be copied like regular data.

HOW TO SAY IT: PORE-ee-gon
IMPERIAL HEIGHT: 2' 07"
METRIC HEIGHT: 0.8m

IMPERIAL WEIGHT: 80.5 lbs.
METRIC WEIGHT: 36.5 kg

POSSIBLE MOVES: Conversion 2, Tackle, Conversion, Sharpen, Psybeam, Agility, Recover, Magnet Rise, Signal Beam, Recycle, Discharge, Lock-On, Tri Attack, Magic Coat, Zap Cannon

Does not evolve

Omanyte
#138
SPIRAL POKÉMON

TYPE: ROCK-WATER

Omanyte's sturdy shell protects it from enemy attacks. This ancient Pokémon was restored from a fossil.

HOW TO SAY IT: AH-man-ite
IMPERIAL HEIGHT: 1' 04"
METRIC HEIGHT: 0.4m

IMPERIAL WEIGHT: 16.5 lbs.
METRIC WEIGHT: 7.5 kg

POSSIBLE MOVES: Constrict, Withdraw, Bite, Water Gun, Rollout, Leer, Mud Shot, Brine, Protect, Ancient Power, Tickle, Rock Blast, Shell Smash, Hydro Pump

EVOLUTION
Omanyte › Omastar

#139
Omastar
SPIRAL POKÉMON

TYPE: ROCK-WATER

Some suspect that Omastar went extinct because it could no longer carry its heavy shell with ease. It seeks out food with its tentacles.

HOW TO SAY IT: AH-mah-star
IMPERIAL HEIGHT: 3' 03"
METRIC HEIGHT: 1.0m

IMPERIAL WEIGHT: 77.2 lbs.
METRIC WEIGHT: 35.0 kg

POSSIBLE MOVES: Constrict, Withdraw, Bite, Water Gun, Rollout, Leer, Mud Shot, Brine, Protect, Ancient Power, Spike, Cannon, Tickle, Rock Blast, Shell Smash, Hydro Pump

EVOLUTION

Omanyte › Omastar

#140
Kabuto
SHELLFISH POKÉMON

TYPE: ROCK-WATER

Kabuto has remained unchanged for 300 million years. It was restored from a fossil, but every once in a while, a living specimen is discovered in the wild.

HOW TO SAY IT: ka-BOO-toe
IMPERIAL HEIGHT: 1' 08"
METRIC HEIGHT: 0.5m

IMPERIAL WEIGHT: 25.4 lbs.
METRIC WEIGHT: 11.5 kg

POSSIBLE MOVES: Scratch, Harden, Absorb, Leer, Mud Shot, Sand Attack, Endure, Aqua Jet, Mega Drain, Metal Sound, Ancient Power, Wring Out

EVOLUTION Kabuto › Kabutops

#141
Kabutops
SHELLFISH POKÉMON

TYPE: ROCK-WATER

Long ago, Kabutops swam through ancient seas in search of food. Its legs and gills were just beginning to adapt to a life on land.

HOW TO SAY IT: KA-boo-tops
IMPERIAL HEIGHT: 4' 03"
METRIC HEIGHT: 1.3m

IMPERIAL WEIGHT: 89.3 lbs.
METRIC WEIGHT: 40.5 kg

POSSIBLE MOVES: Feint, Scratch, Harden, Absorb, Leer, Mud Shot, Sand Attack, Endure, Aqua Jet, Mega Drain, Slash, Metal Sound, Ancient Power, Wring Out, Night Slash

EVOLUTION Kabuto › Kabutops

Aerodactyl

FOSSIL POKÉMON

TYPE: *ROCK-FLYING*

This Pokémon was restored from a piece of fossilized amber. It's said that Aerodactyl ruled the skies in its ancient world.

HOW TO SAY IT: AIR-row-DACK-tull
IMPERIAL HEIGHT: 5' 11"
METRIC HEIGHT: 1.8m

IMPERIAL WEIGHT: 130.1 lbs.
METRIC WEIGHT: 59.0 kg

POSSIBLE MOVES: Iron Head, Ice Fang, Fire Fang, Thunder Fang, Wing Attack, Supersonic, Bite, Scary Face, Roar, Agility, Ancient Power, Crunch, Take Down, Sky Drop, Hyper Beam, Rock Slide, Giga Impact

EVOLUTION

Does not evolve

TYPE: *NORMAL*

Snorlax spends most of its time eating and sleeping. Small children sometimes play by bouncing on this gentle Pokémon's vast belly.

HOW TO SAY IT: **SNOR-lacks**
IMPERIAL HEIGHT: **6' 11"**
METRIC HEIGHT: **2.1m**

IMPERIAL WEIGHT: **1,014.1 lbs.**
METRIC WEIGHT: **460.0 kg**

POSSIBLE MOVES: **Tackle, Defense Curl, Amnesia, Lick, Chip Away, Yawn, Body Slam, Rest, Snore, Sleep Talk, Rollout, Block, Belly Drum, Crunch, Heavy Slam, Giga Impact**

EVOLUTION

Does not evolve

(115)

#144
Articuno
FREEZE POKÉMON

TYPE: ICE-FLYING

When Articuno flaps its wings, the air turns chilly. This Legendary Pokémon often brings snowfall in its wake.

HOW TO SAY IT: ART-tick-COO-no
IMPERIAL HEIGHT: 5' 07"
METRIC HEIGHT: 1.7m
IMPERIAL WEIGHT: 122.1 lbs.
METRIC WEIGHT: 55.4 kg

POSSIBLE MOVES: Roost, Hurricane, Freeze-Dry, Tailwind, Sheer Cold, Gust, Powder Snow, Mist, Ice Shard, Mind Reader, Ancient Power, Agility, Ice Beam, Reflect, Hail, Tailwind, Blizzard

EVOLUTION

Does not evolve

#145
Zapdos
ELECTRIC POKÉMON

TYPE: ELECTRIC-FLYING

When Zapdos is hit by a bolt of lightning, its power increases. This Legendary Pokémon can bend electricity to its will.

HOW TO SAY IT: ZAP-dose
IMPERIAL HEIGHT: 5' 03"
METRIC HEIGHT: 1.6m

IMPERIAL WEIGHT: 116.0 lbs.
METRIC WEIGHT: 52.6 kg

POSSIBLE MOVES: Roost, Zap Cannon, Drill, Peck, Thunder Shock, Thunder Wave, Detect, Pluck, Ancient Power, Charge, Agility, Discharge, Rain Dance, Light Screen, Drill Peck, Thunder

EVOLUTION

Does not evolve

(117)

Moltres

FLAME POKÉMON

TYPE: FIRE-FLYING

When Moltres gets hurt, some say it dives into an active volcano and heals itself by bathing in lava. This Legendary Pokémon can give off flames and control fire.

HOW TO SAY IT: MOL-trays
IMPERIAL HEIGHT: 6' 07"
METRIC HEIGHT: 2.0m

IMPERIAL WEIGHT: 132.3 lbs.
METRIC WEIGHT: 60.0 kg

POSSIBLE MOVES: Roost, Hurricane, Sky Attack, Heat Wave, Wing Attack, Ember, Fire Spin, Agility, Endure, Ancient Power, Flamethrower, Safeguard, Air Slash, Sunny Day, Heat Wave, Solar Beam

Does not evolve

#147
Dratini
DRAGON POKÉMON

TYPE: DRAGON

As Dratini grows, it is constantly in molt, shedding its skin to accommodate the life energy that builds up within it.

HOW TO SAY IT: dra-TEE-nee
IMPERIAL HEIGHT: 5' 11"
METRIC HEIGHT: 1.8m
IMPERIAL WEIGHT: 7.3 lbs.
METRIC WEIGHT: 3.3 kg

POSSIBLE MOVES: Wrap, Leer, Thunder Wave, Twister, Dragon Rage, Slam, Agility, Dragon Tail, Aqua Tail, Dragon Rush, Safeguard, Dragon Dance, Outrage, Hyper Beam

EVOLUTION
Dratini › Dragonair › Dragonite

#148
Dragonair
DRAGON POKÉMON

TYPE: DRAGON

Dragonair's internal energy can be discharged from special crystals on its body. Apparently, when this happens, it can change the local weather.

HOW TO SAY IT: DRAG-gon-AIR
IMPERIAL HEIGHT: 13' 01"
METRIC HEIGHT: 4.0m
IMPERIAL WEIGHT: 36.4 lbs.
METRIC WEIGHT: 16.5 kg

POSSIBLE MOVES: Wrap, Leer, Thunder Wave, Twister, Dragon Rage, Slam, Agility, Dragon Tail, Aqua Tail, Dragon Rush, Safeguard, Dragon Dance, Outrage, Hyper Beam

EVOLUTION
Dratini › Dragonair › Dragonite

Dragonite

DRAGON POKÉMON

TYPE: DRAGON-FLYING

Dragonite can fly around the whole world in less than a day. When it spies a ship in danger on the stormy ocean, it guides the crew safely to land.

HOW TO SAY IT: DRAG-gon-ite
IMPERIAL HEIGHT: 7' 03"
METRIC HEIGHT: 2.2m

IMPERIAL WEIGHT: 463.0 lbs.
METRIC WEIGHT: 210.0 kg

POSSIBLE MOVES: Hurricane, Fire Punch, Thunder Punch, Roost, Wrap, Leer, Thunder Wave, Twister, Dragon Rage, Slam, Agility, Dragon Tail, Aqua Tail, Dragon Rush, Safeguard, Wing Attack, Dragon Dance, Outrage, Hyper Beam

EVOLUTION

Dratini › Dragonair › Dragonite

Mewtwo

GENETIC POKÉMON

LEGENDARY POKÉMON

TYPE: *PSYCHIC*

Scientists created Mewtwo by manipulating its genes. If only they could have given it a sense of compassion . . .

HOW TO SAY IT: MUE-TOO
IMPERIAL HEIGHT: 6' 07"
METRIC HEIGHT: 2.0m

IMPERIAL WEIGHT: 269.0 lbs.
METRIC WEIGHT: 122.0 kg

POSSIBLE MOVES: Confusion, Disable, Barrier, Swift, Future Sight, Psych Up, Miracle Eye, Mist, Psycho Cut, Amnesia, Power Swap, Guard Swap, Psychic, Me First, Recover, Safeguard, Aura Sphere, Psystrike

EVOLUTION

Does not evolve

#151
Mew

NEW SPECIES POKÉMON

TYPE: *PSYCHIC*

It is said that within Mew's cells rests the entirety of the Pokémon genetic code. This Mythical Pokémon can turn invisible to keep others from noticing it.

HOW TO SAY IT: MUE
IMPERIAL HEIGHT: 1' 04"
METRIC HEIGHT: 0.4m

IMPERIAL WEIGHT: 8.8 lbs.
METRIC WEIGHT: 4.0 kg

POSSIBLE MOVES: Pound, Reflect Type, Transform, Mega Punch, Metronome, Psychic, Barrier, Ancient Power, Amnesia, Me First, Baton Pass, Nasty Plot, Aura Sphere

EVOLUTION

Does not evolve

Pokédex ☑ Checklist

How many Pokémon have you caught, Trainer? Mark the ones you've captured on our handy checklist!

- ☐ 001 Bulbasaur
- ☐ 002 Ivysaur
- ☐ 003 Venusaur
- ☐ 004 Charmander
- ☐ 005 Charmeleon
- ☐ 006 Charizard
- ☐ 007 Squirtle
- ☐ 008 Wartortle
- ☐ 009 Blastoise
- ☐ 010 Caterpie
- ☐ 011 Metapod
- ☐ 012 Butterfree
- ☐ 013 Weedle
- ☐ 014 Kakuna
- ☐ 015 Beedrill
- ☐ 016 Pidgey
- ☐ 017 Pidgeotto
- ☐ 018 Pidgeot
- ☐ 019 Rattata
- ☐ 020 Raticate
- ☐ 021 Spearow
- ☐ 022 Fearow
- ☐ 023 Ekans
- ☐ 024 Arbok
- ☐ 025 Pikachu
- ☐ 026 Raichu
- ☐ 027 Sandshrew

- ☐ 028 Sandslash
- ☐ 029 Nidoran ♀
- ☐ 030 Nidorina
- ☐ 031 Nidoqueen
- ☐ 032 Nidoran ♂
- ☐ 033 Nidorino
- ☐ 034 Nidoking
- ☐ 035 Clefairy
- ☐ 036 Clefable
- ☐ 037 Vulpix
- ☐ 038 Ninetales
- ☐ 039 Jigglypuff
- ☐ 040 Wigglytuff
- ☐ 041 Zubat
- ☐ 042 Golbat
- ☐ 043 Oddish
- ☐ 044 Gloom
- ☐ 045 Vileplume
- ☐ 046 Paras
- ☐ 047 Parasect
- ☐ 048 Venonat
- ☐ 049 Venomoth
- ☐ 050 Diglett
- ☐ 051 Dugtrio
- ☐ 052 Meowth
- ☐ 053 Persian
- ☐ 054 Psyduck

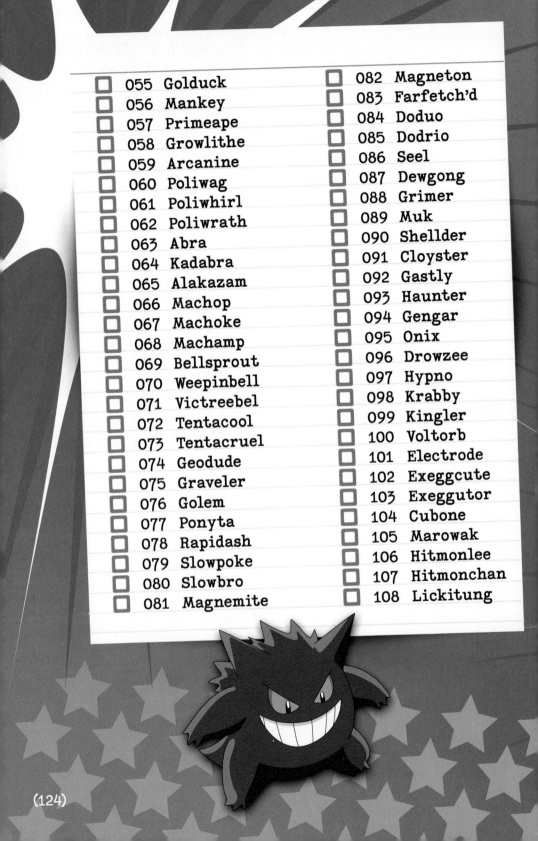

☐ 055 Golduck
☐ 056 Mankey
☐ 057 Primeape
☐ 058 Growlithe
☐ 059 Arcanine
☐ 060 Poliwag
☐ 061 Poliwhirl
☐ 062 Poliwrath
☐ 063 Abra
☐ 064 Kadabra
☐ 065 Alakazam
☐ 066 Machop
☐ 067 Machoke
☐ 068 Machamp
☐ 069 Bellsprout
☐ 070 Weepinbell
☐ 071 Victreebel
☐ 072 Tentacool
☐ 073 Tentacruel
☐ 074 Geodude
☐ 075 Graveler
☐ 076 Golem
☐ 077 Ponyta
☐ 078 Rapidash
☐ 079 Slowpoke
☐ 080 Slowbro
☐ 081 Magnemite

☐ 082 Magneton
☐ 083 Farfetch'd
☐ 084 Doduo
☐ 085 Dodrio
☐ 086 Seel
☐ 087 Dewgong
☐ 088 Grimer
☐ 089 Muk
☐ 090 Shellder
☐ 091 Cloyster
☐ 092 Gastly
☐ 093 Haunter
☐ 094 Gengar
☐ 095 Onix
☐ 096 Drowzee
☐ 097 Hypno
☐ 098 Krabby
☐ 099 Kingler
☐ 100 Voltorb
☐ 101 Electrode
☐ 102 Exeggcute
☐ 103 Exeggutor
☐ 104 Cubone
☐ 105 Marowak
☐ 106 Hitmonlee
☐ 107 Hitmonchan
☐ 108 Lickitung

☐	109	Koffing	☐	131	Lapras
☐	110	Weezing	☐	132	Ditto
☐	111	Rhyhorn	☐	133	Eevee
☐	112	Rhydon	☐	134	Vaporeon
☐	113	Chansey	☐	135	Jolteon
☐	114	Tangela	☐	136	Flareon
☐	115	Kangaskhan	☐	137	Porygon
☐	116	Horsea	☐	138	Omanyte
☐	117	Seadra	☐	139	Omastar
☐	118	Goldeen	☐	140	Kabuto
☐	119	Seaking	☐	141	Kabutops
☐	120	Staryu	☐	142	Aerodactyl
☐	121	Starmie	☐	143	Snorlax
☐	122	Mr. Mime	☐	144	Articuno
☐	123	Scyther	☐	145	Zapdos
☐	124	Jynx	☐	146	Moltres
☐	125	Electabuzz	☐	147	Dratini
☐	126	Magmar	☐	148	Dragonair
☐	127	Pinsir	☐	149	Dragonite
☐	128	Tauros	☐	150	Mewtwo
☐	129	Magikarp	☐	151	Mew
☐	130	Gyarados			

Index

Farewell

Thanks for reading this book, Trainer! Best of luck on your Pokémon journey.